WAR AND DESTINY

RUSSIA AND UKRAINE

by
LARRY KRIEGER

WAR AND DESTINY
RUSSIA AND UKRAINE

by LARRY KRIEGER

ISBN: 978-1-7368182-7-5

A publication of Larry Prep LLC

Art Direction & Design by Station16 (Station16 LLC)

© Copyright 2023 Larry Krieger

All rights reserved.

No part of this book may be used or reproduced in any manner without written permission from the publisher.

For more about the author or this book please visit

www.waranddestinybook.com

PREFACE

The Finnish Prime Minister Sanna Marin admitted that no one knows when the war between Ukraine and Russia will end. But she bluntly warned, "Ukraine has to win. I don't see any other choice."

Prime Minister Marin is right. The war in Ukraine is about more than often obscure borders in eastern Ukraine. It is both a moral fight against unbridled Russian brutality and a battle for the future of global freedom.

If Ukraine must win, then Russian President Vladimir Putin must lose. A Russian victory would embolden dictators in Iran, North Korea, and China. For example, Chinese President Xi Jinping might conclude that the rewards of invading Taiwan would outweigh the costs.

Despite the importance of defeating Russian aggression and defending freedom, public backing for aiding Ukraine has begun to waver. As of this writing, polls report that support among Republicans has fallen from 80 percent in March to just above half.

The polls reflect a worrisome sign of impatience combined with a lack of understanding of what is at stake in Ukraine. I wrote this book to address these problems. The book is not written for scholars. Instead, it is intended to help concerned citizens understand the causes of the war and why it is important to the Free World.

I also wrote the book for Alla Kuznietsova, a 52-year- old Ukrainian woman who lived in Izium. Russian occupiers arrested and repeatedly subjected her to unspeakable acts of torture. But they could not break her spirit. Ms. Kuznietsova survived and told a reporter: "We are grateful to America, but we just ask, please don't leave us halfway. Don't leave us alone."

The book is dedicated to Ms. Kuznietsova and the other courageous Ukrainians who are sacrificing everything to defend the democratic values we hold dear. I hope readers of this book will voice support for Ukraine and not leave its brave people alone.

TABLE OF CONTENTS

PREFACE	III
ABOUT THE AUTHOR	VII
ACKNOWLEDGEMENTS	VII
CHRONOLOGY OF KEY EVENTS	IX
MAPS	XI

CHAPTER 1 — 1
WHY UKRAINE MATTERS

CHAPTER 2 — 5
A NEW WORLD

CHAPTER 3 — 9
PUTIN'S CHARACTER AND RISE TO POWER

CHAPTER 4 — 15
WHY CAN'T WE BE FRIENDS?

CHAPTER 5 — 19
UKRAINE – THE LAND AND THE PEOPLE

CHAPTER 6 — 23
A NEW UKRAINE, 1991–2014

CHAPTER 7 — 31
THE EMPIRE STRIKES BACK, 2014 – 2019

CHAPTER 8 — 39
"DON'T TRUST PUTIN"

CHAPTER 9 — 47
THE BATTLE FOR KYIV

CHAPTER 10 — 55
THE HUMAN FRONT: ATROCITIES AND REFUGEES

CHAPTER 11	**63**
THE ECONOMIC FRONT: SANCTIONS AND ENERGY	
CHAPTER 12	**71**
THE INFORMATION FRONT: PROPAGANDA AND MISINFORMATION	
CHAPTER 13	**79**
MR. PUTIN'S WAR: APRIL – SEPTEMBER 2022	
CHAPTER 14	**87**
FOREVER OR NEVER	
CHAPTER 15	**93**
SIX LESSONS FROM THE UKRAINE WAR	
KEY PEOPLE, PLACES, AND TERMS	**101**

ABOUT THE AUTHOR

Larry Krieger earned his B.A. and M.A.T. from the University of North Carolina at Chapel Hill and his M.A. from Wake Forest. In a career spanning more than four decades, Mr. Krieger taught in urban, rural, and suburban public schools in North Carolina and New Jersey.

Mr. Krieger has taken great pride in helping his students understand complex subjects. He has taught a variety of AP subjects including U.S. History, Art History, European History, and American Government. Mr. Krieger has published popular books in all of these subjects.

Mr. Krieger's AP courses were renowned for the energetic presentations, commitment to scholarship, and dedication to helping students achieve high AP exam scores. The College Board recognized Mr. Krieger's classroom excellence by naming him the world's most successful AP Art History teacher for two straight years. Mr. Krieger has never had an AP student score a one or a two.

ACKNOWLEDGEMENTS

Books do not write themselves. They require the work and inspiration of a number of dedicated and creative people.

The typed manuscript must be proofed and assembled into an attractive and well-designed book. As always, Station16 more than met this challenge. Brenton played a key leadership role. He offered valuable advice, and managed the project to a successful conclusion. David carefully proofed each page, Ana shaped the manuscript into flowing layouts, and Michael and Stacy developed a distinctive cover design.

This book began with a series of daily Commentaries on the Ukraine War. I owe a special thanks to Carl Florczyk and his Contemporary Issues students at Freeburg High School. Carl turned each Commentary into a successful lesson. His positive response encouraged me to write this book.

Prasad Vinnakota is the Director of the Sigma Academy in Montgomery, New Jersey. Prasad listened to my weekly reports detailing the book's ongoing progress and encouraged me to keep reading, organizing, and writing.

I would especially like to thank Toni Alexander for reading and commenting on each chapter. Toni's encouragement helped motivate me to read and synthesize over a dozen books and hundreds of news and magazine articles.

I owe a special thank you to my brother, Dr. Gary Krieger. Gary read and critiqued each chapter. Our almost daily conversations helped to clarify complex issues and shape the book's organization.

And finally, I owe an extra special thank you to my wife Susan for her dedication to this project. As "Editor-in-Chief" Susan read, critiqued, and proofed every page in this book. Her "close reads" spotted misplaced modifiers, passive voice verbs, and unconnected thoughts. Susan gave every chapter a grade and always encouraged me to be "clear and direct."

CHRONOLOGY OF KEY EVENTS

AUGUST 24, 1991

Ukraine declares its independence

DECEMBER 31, 1999

Boris Yeltsin resigns and appoints Vladimir Putin president of Russia

DECEMBER 2004

Orange Revolution in Ukraine begins

NOVEMBER 21, 2013

Revolution of Dignity in Ukraine begins

FEBRUARY 27, 2014

Unmarked Russian special forces ("Little Green Men") begin to takeover government buildings and airports in Crimea

APRIL – MAY, 2014

War in the Donbas begins

MAY 20, 2019

Volodymyr Zelensky is sworn in as Ukraine's sixth president

FEBRUARY 24, 2022

Russia begins an all-out invasion of Ukraine

SEPTEMBER 21, 2022

Vladimir Putin calls for a partial mobilization of 300,000 troops

SEPTEMBER 30, 2022

Vladimir Putin formally annexes Luhansk, Donetsk, Kherson, and Zaporizhia saying they will become part of Russia "forever"

NOVEMBER 11, 2022
Ukrainian forces liberate Kherson

DECEMBER 21, 2022
Volodymyr Zelensky addresses a joint session of Congress

FEBRUARY 20, 2023
President Biden meets with President Zelensky in Kyiv

MAPS
EUROPE

UKRAINE

KHERSON REGION

CRIMEA PENINSULA

DONBAS REGION

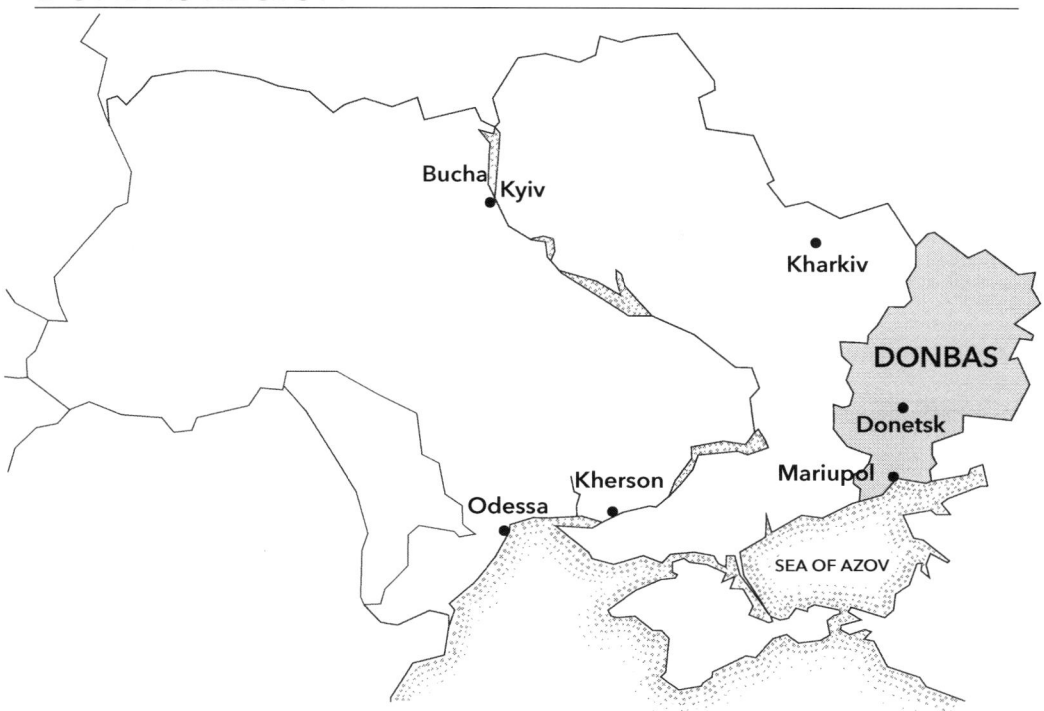

CHAPTER 1
WHY UKRAINE MATTERS

CHAPTER 1
WHY UKRAINE MATTERS

On January 1, 2022, Americans celebrated the beginning of a New Year. Many enjoyed watching New Year's Day parades and watching college football games. As the New Year began, few Americans could locate Ukraine on a map or identify its distinctive yellow and blue flag. But this suddenly changed on February 24 when Russian President Vladimir Putin launched an unprovoked attack on Ukraine.

Russia's brutal invasion and the resulting humanitarian crisis stunned the world. Shocking and painful images of bombed buildings, terrified refugees, and mass graves dominated the news. The crisis forced both global leaders and the American public to come to grips with one pressing question: "Why does the fate of Ukraine matter?'

The answers to this question are crucial to understanding this pivotal historic moment. The war is obviously crucial for Ukraine. But the conflict is not just about Ukraine. It will have immense consequences for democratic values and for America's role as the leader of the Free World.

UKRAINE MATTERS BECAUSE WE CAN'T ALLOW MIGHT TO MAKE RIGHT

Does "might make right"? For most of human history the answer has been yes. In his classic account of the Peloponnesian War between Athens and Sparta, the Greek historian Thucydides wrote, "The strong do what they can and the weak suffer what they must."

Thucydides's grim but realistic prediction proved to be accurate. For centuries, aggressive nations and their ambitious rulers used force to conquer weaker nations. But this brutal and enduring characteristic of power politics seemed to change in the decades following World War II. Shocked by the war's devastation, European and American leaders created a new rules-based international order in which accepted borders would not be changed by force.

This norm against territorial conquest brought Europe seven decades of peace and prosperity. But Vladimir Putin did not share this vision. He later described the collapse of the Soviet Union as "the greatest geopolitical catastrophe of the century." Humiliated by the unraveling of the Soviet Union, Putin vowed to restore Russia's global position of power and influence.

Putin began to challenge the norm against territorial conquest in Ukraine. In 2014, he annexed Ukraine's Crimean Peninsula and then carved out semi-autonomous republics in a region of eastern Ukraine known as the Donbas. Putin's unprovoked invasion of Ukraine represents a blatant attempt to create a new international order based upon force. Ukraine matters because Putin cannot be allowed to redraw the map of Europe and might cannot be allowed to make right.

UKRAINE MATTERS BECAUSE DICTATORS CANNOT BE APPEASED

Hitler was a ruthless and amoral dictator who threatened to reverse the restrictions placed upon Germany by the Versailles Treaty. During the 1930s, Britain and France hoped that making territorial concessions would keep the peace. Known as appeasement, this misguided policy emboldened Hitler and led to World War II. In the years following the Second World War, appeasement became synonymous with surrender. American and European leaders vowed they would never again appease dictators.

Like Hitler, Vladimir Putin is a ruthless and amoral dictator. Undeterred by the threat of economic sanctions, Putin ordered the Russian war machine to invade Ukraine. Recalling the lessons of appeasing Hitler, Estonian Prime Minister Kaja Kallas warned, "If Putin wins, or even has a view that he has won this war, his appetite will only grow." The outspoken Putin critic Garry Kasparov underscored Kallas' warning when he bluntly reminded Americans and Europeans, "Evil doesn't die."

Kallas and Kasparov are both right. If Putin's aggression is allowed to go unchecked, it will embolden other authoritarian leaders. For example, President Xi Jinping of China may conclude that the gains of invading Taiwan outweigh the costs. Ukraine matters because the price of allowing Putin's treacherous aggression is too high. Ukraine matters because it reminds us that dictators cannot be appeased.

UKRAINE MATTERS BECAUSE DEMOCRACY MATTERS

Putin's invasion of Ukraine is taking place in the context of a global contest between democracies and autocracies. Democracy values regard for human rights, the rule of law, and the freedom of individuals to think, act, and create. Putin fears that a democratic and prosperous Ukraine on Russia's border would inevitably pose a threat to his autocratic and corrupt rule.

The United States is the leader of the Free World. In his inaugural address, President Kennedy pledged the United States would "pay any price, bear any burden, meet any hardship, support any friend, oppose any foe to assure the survival and the success of liberty." He concluded by embracing "the role of defending freedom in its hour of maximum danger."

America now faces another hour of "maximum danger." Putin cannot be allowed to destroy Ukraine's democratically elected government. Americans have always taken democracy seriously. Ukraine matters because democracy matters.

CHAPTER 2
A NEW WORLD

CHAPTER 2
A NEW WORLD

Mikhail Gorbachev became the General Secretary of the Communist Party of the Soviet Union in 1985. At that time the Soviet Union was the world's most feared totalitarian dictatorship. But Gorbachev quickly recognized that "something was wrong." He surprised traditionalists inside the Kremlin by launching a bold program of reforms designed to revitalize the Soviet Union's rigid political and economic system.

Gorbachev's new policy of glasnost, or openness, brought a series of unprecedented changes. Soviet citizens were encouraged to speak, write, and worship freely. And for the first time in Soviet history, citizens were allowed to vote in free elections.

Gorbachev's "new thinking" also brought sweeping foreign policy changes. He allowed the Berlin Wall to fall, freed Eastern Europe, accepted German reunification, and slowed the nuclear arms race. As a result of these changes the Cold War began to thaw and then melt away.

"THINGS ARE HAPPENING SO QUICKLY"

The new spirit of openness also began to affect the Soviet Union's 15 republics. These republics had been held together by a combination of fear and force. But the new taste of freedom encouraged the republics to demand greater independence from Moscow.

The first challenge to Soviet stability occurred in Lithuania, Estonia, and Latvia. Known as the Baltic states, these three republics had been independent nations between the two world wars. However, the 1939 Nazi-Soviet Pact enabled Stalin to brutally annex all three Baltic countries.

Ignoring Gorbachev's pleas for restraint, the Lithuanian Parliament declared the republic's independence from the Soviet Union on March 11, 1990. Inspired by Lithuania, both Estonia and Latvia also declared their unconditional independence. "Things are happening so quickly," said one amazed Estonia official. "We are taking advantage of opportunities we did not have before."

The drive toward independence from the Soviet Union soon spread to Ukraine. Gorbachev recognized that Ukraine was an indispensable part of the Soviet Union. Its population of about 50 million people made it the nation's second most populous republic. Ukraine's thriving factories produced about one-quarter of the Soviet Union's industrial output while its fertile fields produced almost half of the country's agricultural products.

Convinced that independence offered a better life, Ukraine's leaders ignored Gorbachev's desperate pleas to remain in the Soviet Union. On December 1, 1991, 92.3 percent of Ukrainian voters overwhelmingly approved a referendum for independence. "This is a good day," rejoiced one voter, "It is the flowering of our soul."

"WE'RE NOW LIVING IN A NEW WORLD"

Independence movements in the Baltic states and Ukraine created an irreversible momentum. By late 1991, all 15 Soviet republics declared their independence. Gorbachev had become a leader without a country.

Gorbachev chose to resign on December 25, 1991. After proudly reviewing his accomplishments, he told a nationally televised audience, "We're now living in a new world." Gorbachev was right. A few moments after his resignation, Kremlin guards lowered the Soviet flag for the last time. The red flag bearing the distinctive gold hammer-and-sickle emblem had flown over the Kremlin since Lenin seized power in 1917. The guards then raised the white, red, and blue flag of the Russian Republic. Chimes from the Kremlin's tower rang for several minutes to mark the historic event. The Soviet Union passed into history, and a new era seemed to begin.

The great stream of history is often unpredictable. The death of the Soviet Union appeared to signal the end of the Cold War and the beginning of what President George H.W. Bush called "a new world order." No one would have predicted that the brief respite from Cold War tensions would end when an obscure former deputy mayor of St. Petersburg named Vladimir Putin became the new Russian president on the last day of 1999.

CHAPTER 3
PUTIN'S CHARACTER AND RISE TO POWER

CHAPTER 3
PUTIN'S CHARACTER AND RISE TO POWER

Who is Vladimir Putin? What character traits define his personality and guide his decisions? How did he rise from the streets of war-torn Leningrad (now St. Petersburg) to the pinnacle of power in Moscow? The answers to these questions can be found in a combination of key personal experiences and pivotal historic events that shaped Putin's character and transformed him into one of the world's most dangerous and formidable leaders.

THE CORNERED RAT IN LENINGRAD

Vladimir Putin was born in 1952 in Leningrad. His working-class parents barely survived the brutal Nazi siege of the once prosperous city. The Putin family lived in a 215-square foot room inside a communal building with a stove in the hallway and a bathroom in the stairwell. Putin called this place home until he was 25 years old.

As a young boy Putin faced a constant battle for survival. He later recalled using a stick to chase rats around his dismal apartment building: "Once I spotted a huge rat and pursued it down the hall until I drove it into a corner. It had nowhere to run. Suddenly it lashed around and threw itself at me…Now the rat was chasing me."

This vivid incident shaped Putin's outlook on life and war. He concluded that if cornered he must resolve to "fight to the finish" and attack his opponents like the cornered rat in his childhood story.

JUDO – "A MUST FOR A POLITICIAN"

Leningrad's mean streets forced Putin to become a fighter. Standing just 5 feet 7 inches tall, Putin turned to judo as a way of defending himself from neighborhood bullies. The strategy worked. Putin's growing competence won the respect of teammates who admired his ability to use cunning and surprise to defeat much bigger opponents. Although he weighed just 135 pounds, Putin became Leningrad's judo champion in 1976.

Judo did more than enable Putin to win trophies; it also shaped his character. Years of practice helped Putin learn how to exploit an opponent's hesitation or temporary disorientation. His favorite move was the deashibari, a swift attack designed to knock an opponent off his feet. Putin later confided to an interviewer that judo taught him to "be in control, to feel the sharpness of the moment, to see strong and weak points of the opponent…skills that are simply a must for a politician."

KGB OPERATIVE

Putin's status as a judo champion helped motivate him to become a more disciplined and ambitious student. He successfully attended law school at Leningrad State University. After graduating in 1975, Putin joined the KGB. As the Soviet Union's feared security agency, the KGB specialized in obtaining intelligence, protecting national security, and suppressing domestic dissent.

Putin worked for the KGB for 16 years. During this time, he prided himself on becoming a "specialist in human relations" who could quickly evaluate an individual's motivations and needs. Putin soon became a master manipulator adept at deceiving and misleading both friends and adversaries. CNN's Moscow Bureau Chief later recalled Putin's ability to "reflect back to the person with whom he is interacting whatever that person wants to hear. If it's someone polite, Putin can be polite. If it's someone rough or crude, Putin can use profanity and off-color language better than any politician I've seen."

"MOSCOW IS SILENT"

In 1985, the KGB assigned Putin to work in its intelligence unit located in Dresden, East Germany. He watched with growing alarm as huge crowds of jubilant Berliners slammed hammers into the wall and shouted, "The wall is gone!" Now that the unthinkable had occurred, protests spread to Dresden as demonstrators hoped to destroy other visible symbols of communist authority.

On December 5, 1989 an angry crowd gathered outside KGB headquarters in Dresden. Fearing that the demonstrators would burst into the building,

Putin placed urgent calls to his superiors in Moscow. After several unanswered calls, he was finally told, "We cannot do anything without orders from Moscow. And Moscow is silent."

Recognizing that he was on his own, Putin walked outside to confront the mob. He falsely claimed that armed guards inside the building would fire on any trespassers. His carefully calculated bluff worked. However, the incident left Putin with an enduring fear of popular uprisings.

THE COLLAPSE OF SOVIET AUTHORITY

While the world celebrated the fall of the Berlin Wall as a triumph of democracy, Putin viewed it as a humiliating disaster. From his point of view, the Soviet Union's geopolitical crisis became even worse when all 15 of its republics declared their independence.

The sudden demise of the Soviet Union seemed to vindicate America's Cold War policy of containment. President George H.W. Bush envisioned a "new world order" where American leadership would promote democracy, the rule of law, and economic growth. But Putin did not share Bush's vision. He later described the collapse of the Soviet Union as "the greatest geopolitical catastrophe of the century."

A METEORIC RISE TO POWER

The Soviet Union's sudden collapse stunned Putin. Uncertain what to do, he returned to Leningrad and briefly considered an academic career as an economist. However, he soon plunged into politics by helping his former law professor, Anatoly Sobchak, become the first democratically elected mayor of the now renamed city of St. Petersburg.

Sobchak rewarded Putin's hard work and loyalty by appointing him deputy mayor. However, Sobchak's failure to win reelection in 1996 appeared to be a serious setback for Putin's political aspirations. But events then took an unexpected turn.

Putin's calmness under stress and willingness to make pragmatic decisions attracted the attention of key figures in the administration of Russian President Boris Yeltsin. Offered a job by a top Kremlin official, Putin sensed an opportunity and moved to Moscow.

While Putin's political career steadily advanced, Russia experienced a tumultuous period of soaring inflation and political instability. "I had the feeling," Putin later recalled, "that the country was no more. It had disappeared…I wanted something different to rise in its place."

Putin soon had an opportunity to achieve his goal. Yeltsin viewed Putin as a loyal, energetic, and strong leader. On December 31, 1999, Yeltsin shocked the world by resigning his office and naming Putin acting president of Russia. Less than three months later, Russian voters officially elected Putin to a four-year term as President. The election completed Putin's improbable and meteoric rise from the streets of war-torn Leningrad to the pinnacle of power in Moscow. The world would soon discover that Putin was a ruthless and calculating leader determined to restore Russia's status as a great power.

CHAPTER 4

WHY CAN'T WE BE FRIENDS?

CHAPTER 4
WHY CAN'T WE BE FRIENDS?

The 30 guests at President George W. Bush's Texas ranch were enjoying a dinner that included "a little Texas barbecue, pecan pie, a little Texas music." Bush then offered a toast to his honored guest, Russian President Vladimir Putin: "Usually you only invite good friends to your home and this is clearly the case here." President Putin thanked his host and looked forward to the removal of the "dead weights we inherited from the Cold War."

Held on November 15 – 16, 2002, the Texas summit marked the high point of post-Cold War U.S.-Soviet relations. Relying on goodwill and personal relationships could not remove the "dead weights" from America and Russia's very different historic experiences and outlooks on global affairs.

THE INFLUENCE OF GEOGRAPHY

Abraham Lincoln recognized the security provided by America's unique geographic location when he noted, "All the armies of Europe, Asia, and Africa combined, with all the treasures of the earth (our own excepted) in their military chest, with a Bonaparte for a commander, could not by force take a drink from the Ohio or make a track on the Blue Ridge in a trial of a thousand years." Lincoln was right. The combination of vast oceans on America's eastern and western borders and weak but friendly nations to the North and South have guaranteed America security from invasion.

Russia's geographic location offers a stark contrast. Russia occupies a huge land mass that stretches across eleven time zones. Unlike the United States, no natural barriers define Russia's borders. While the United States takes its security for granted, Russia has never known a friendly neighbor. During the Thirteenth and Fourteenth centuries, Mongols from the east swept across Russia. In 1812, Napoleon Bonaparte's Grand Army invaded Russia and briefly captured Moscow. Less than a century later, Japan attacked and invaded territories in eastern Russia. And Germany invaded Russia twice during the first half of the twentieth century.

This vivid incident shaped Putin's outlook on life and war. He concluded that if cornered he must resolve to "fight to the finish" and attack his opponents like the cornered rat in his childhood story.

INDIVIDUAL RIGHTS VERSUS CENTRALIZED POWER

Eighteenth century Enlightenment thought deeply influenced America's founders. They prized reason and rejected intolerance. The Declaration of Independence forthrightly declared that "life, liberty, and the pursuit of happiness" are God-given natural rights. America's democratic culture stressed individual freedom and the sanctity of life.

The Enlightenment had little impact on Russian society. Ravaged by wars, Russia turned to a powerful centralized government to protect it from hostile neighbors. Both Russia's tsars and its Twentieth century Communist Party rulers suppressed individual rights and the rule of law. Instead, they created a pyramid of power that demanded blind obedience from their subjugated people.

DIFFERING APPROACHES TO FOREIGN POLICY

Secure from external threats and blessed with abundant natural resources, the United States has taken its security for granted. America's geographic advantages and cultural traditions of individual liberty and limited government have shaped a unique approach to foreign policy. In his 2005 Inaugural Address, President George W. Bush summarized America's historic mission when he declared, "It is the policy of the United States to seek and support the growth of democratic movements and institutions in every nation and culture, with the ultimate goal of ending tyranny in our world."

Russian leaders do not share Bush's idealistic vision of foreign policy. Their historic experience has taught them that peace is not a natural or normal condition. This awareness of danger has produced ruthless leaders who trust no one and are always suspiciously alert. Russian foreign policy thus places no faith in the possibility of a permanent peaceful coexistence between rival powers.

"WE CANNOT – EVER – BE FRIENDS"

Vladimir Putin is following Russia's traditional assertive policy of international relations. Convinced that might makes right, Putin views moral principles and mutual expressions of goodwill as signs of weakness that can and should be exploited. The Lithuanian writer Kristina Sabaliauskaite reminds her readers that in Putin's worldview there is no rule of law. Instead, "the world is just a cake to be sliced by those who happen to hold a knife."

Rebekah Koffler shares Sabaliauskaite's sense of growing peril. Koffler is a Russian-born U.S. intelligence expert. In her book, Putin's Playbook, she warns that Russia and the United States are on "a geopolitical collision course." Koeffler forcefully concludes with this emphatic statement: "We cannot – ever – be friends."

CHAPTER 5

UKRAINE – THE LAND AND THE PEOPLE

CHAPTER 5
UKRAINE – THE LAND AND THE PEOPLE

Look closely at the map of Europe on page XI. Ukraine is hard to miss. It's Europe's second largest country after Russia. With an area of 233,100 square miles, Ukraine is larger than France but a bit smaller than Texas.

Ukraine shares borders with seven countries and two seas. It borders Poland, Slovakia, and Hungary in the west, Moldova and Romania in the southwest, Belarus in the north, Russia in the east, and the Black Sea and Sea of Azov in the south.

"THE BREADBASKET OF THE WORLD"

Ukraine's topography is not complex. Almost the entire country consists of vast fertile plains. Rich black earth covers two-thirds of Ukraine. This abundant resource has made Ukraine one of the world's most important agricultural regions.

Ukraine's productive farms justify the country's reputation as "the breadbasket of the world." The world relies on Ukraine for about 14 percent of its corn, 10 percent of its wheat, and 17 percent of its barley. In addition, Ukraine is the world's largest exporter of sunflower oil and its fourth largest exporter of potatoes.

MINERAL RESOURCES

Nature has endowed Ukraine with impressive mineral resources. A region in eastern Ukraine known as the Donbas contains rich deposits of iron ore and coal. The close proximity of these minerals has enabled Ukraine to become the world's tenth largest producer of steel. The heavy industries located in the Donbas supported about a quarter of the Soviet Union's military-industrial complex.

MAJOR CITIES

Kyiv is Ukraine's capital and most populous city. It is located in north-central Ukraine along the banks of the Dnipro River. Kyiv is home to nearly 3 million people, making it Europe's seventh most populous city. It is renowned for its historic monuments, impressive museums, and golden-domed churches.

Lviv is located in western Ukraine about 40 miles from the Polish border. The city's university has made it a center of progressive political ideas. About 1,500 cafes line the winding streets in Lviv's quaint historic district.

Odessa is a major warm water port located on the northwestern shore of the Black Sea. The city's harbor facilities handle the majority of Ukraine's imports and exports. Known as the "Pearl by the Sea," Odessa features beaches and boulevards popular with tourists.

Kharkiv is Ukraine's second largest city. It is located in northeastern Ukraine just 20 miles from the Russian border. Kharkiv is a major cultural, transportation, and industrial center.

REGIONAL DIFFERENCES

Geographic and historical differences have divided Ukraine into the following four distinctive regions:

1. Western Ukraine – This region includes the city of Lviv and the small towns and resorts in the Carpathian Mountains. The region was controlled by the Austrian-Hungarian Empire and did not become a recognized part of Soviet Ukraine until 1944.
2. Central Ukraine – This region lies on either side of the Dnipro River. It includes Kyiv as well as rich farming lands.
3. Eastern Ukraine – This region includes the heavily-industrialized region known as the Donbas.
4. Southern Ukraine – This region includes Odessa, lands bordering the Black Sea, and the Crimean Peninsula.

ETHNIC AND LINGUISTIC DIFFERENCES

Ethnic and linguistic differences have played an important role in shaping Ukrainian attitudes toward their national identity and relationship with the European Union and Russia.

In 2001, roughly 77.5 percent of Ukraine's population identified as ethnic Ukrainians. With 17.2 percent of the population, ethnic Russians comprised the second largest group. They clustered in urban areas in the eastern and southern regions of the country.

Language also divided Ukrainians into two regional groups. People living in western and central parts of the country typically identified Ukrainian as their native language. In contrast, Ukrainians living in the east and south typically identified Russian as their native language.

These ethnic and linguistic divisions coincide with important political differences. Ukrainians living in the western and the central portions of the country have favored closer ties with nations in the European Union. However, Ukrainians living in the east and south have favored closer ties with Russia.

CHAPTER 6
A NEW UKRAINE, 1991–2014

CHAPTER 6
A NEW UKRAINE, 1991–2014

The moment Levko Lukianenko had worked and suffered towards had finally arrived. A Ukrainian patriot and Soviet dissident, Lukianenko had been a political prisoner for 26 years in a gulag, or forced-labor camp. Now an elected member of the Ukrainian parliament, Rada, he was chosen to write a document declaring Ukrainian independence from the Soviet Union.

Eager to separate from a country he had once branded as "the greatest evil of present-day life," Lukianenko rose to the challenge. His short but forceful document forthrightly stated, "In view of the deadly threat posed to our country…and continuing the thousand-year-old tradition of state building in Ukraine…the Rada solemnly proclaims the Independence of Ukraine…From now on only the Constitution and laws of Ukraine will be in force on its territory."

On August 24, 1991, jubilant Rada deputies overwhelmingly endorsed Lukianenko's declaration. A popular referendum held three months later confirmed the Rada's decision with more than 90 percent of voters supporting independence.

What had seemed an impossibility had now become a reality. Ukraine was an independent country free to chart its own path into the future. But its leaders and people faced daunting challenges. They would have to find a way to part with Ukraine's Soviet past while also maintaining a precarious relationship with both Europe and Russia.

"A NEW UKRAINE HAS BEEN BORN"

On December 1, 1991, Ukrainian voters selected Leonid Kravchuk as their country's first democratically elected president. Kravchuk proudly proclaimed, "A new Ukraine has been born." As a former Communist

Party leader, he had earned a reputation as a "wily fox" who could steal a chicken without upsetting the farmer.

A group of interrelated problems quickly tested Kravchuk's political skills. He successfully began Ukraine's transition from a Soviet republic to an independent country. At the same he carefully balanced Ukraine's diverse regional attitudes towards Russia. Despite these achievements, he could not prevent the collapse of Ukraine's economy.

During the Soviet era, bureaucrats in Moscow ran Ukraine's industrial and agricultural enterprises. Meaningful reforms would require ending subsidies to inefficient factories and farms that would force thousands of workers to lose their jobs. The failure of the Kravchuk government to enact needed reforms created a severe economic depression. By the end of 1993, inflation soared to 70 percent per month while Ukraine's Gross Domestic Product (GDP) plummeted by over 30 percent.

Living conditions in Ukraine resembled those in America during the depths of the Great Depression. Frustrated consumers found empty shops while unemployed workers found locked factory gates. A nation renowned as Europe's breadbasket had become an economic failure in which 85 percent of the population lived below the poverty line.

The economic crisis doomed Kravchuk's popularity. In 1994, voters rejected his bid for a second presidential term. Although he lost the election, Kravchuk established a precedent for a peaceful transfer of power by stepping aside for his successor, Leonid Kuchma.

KUCHMA AND CORRUPTION

Kuchma successfully enacted measures that ended Ukraine's hyperinflation. The country's rising middle-class hoped Kuchma would promote a new era of economic modernization. Instead, he supported a group of ambitious, ruthless, and corrupt businessmen known in Ukraine, as in Russia, as oligarchs.

The oligarchs successfully stymied economic reforms. Corruption soon became a pervasive part of doing business in Ukraine. For example, a Spanish entrepreneur had to pay for four licenses and obtain the signatures of twenty-five people before he could export a shipload of sunflower seeds. But that was not all: the outraged businessman later complained, "I'm paying one high-up guy's son a salary, and next week somebody else's kids are going on holiday to Spain, out of my pocket."

Public outrage at widespread government corruption weakened support for Kuchma's administration. His downfall accelerated when a bodyguard released 300 hours of tapes secretly recorded in Kuchma's presidential office. Known as "Kuchmagate," the recordings revealed that Kuchma accepted bribes, suppressed opposition media, and was implicated in the death of a prominent investigative reporter.

YANUKOVYCH VERSUS YUSHCHENKO

Kuchma's term of office ended in January 2005. The presidential election offered Ukrainian voters a choice between two very different candidates.

Viktor Yanukovych experienced hard times as a youth growing up in an industrial area in eastern Ukraine. He later recalled, "I walked around bare-footed in the streets. I had to fight for myself every day." After serving a pair of jail terms for robbery and assault, Yanukovych turned his life around by beginning a successful career as a transportation executive. His unpolished manner did not prevent Yanukovych from becoming a popular regional political leader who developed close ties with President Kuchma. As Kuchma's Prime Minister from 2002 – 2005, Yanukovych endorsed pro-Russian foreign policies while ignoring the corrupt practices of Ukraine's powerful oligarchs.

Viktor Yushchenko's life experiences and political ideas offered a marked contrast with those of Yanukovych. Raised by professional educators in a predominantly Ukrainian-speaking region in northeastern Ukraine, Yushchenko valued education. After graduating from college, he launched a successful career as a central banker. He developed a reputation as a populist who opposed corruption, supported free-market capitalism, and endorsed closer ties with Western democracies.

THE ORANGE REVOLUTION

Supporters of Yanukovych and Yushchenko waged vigorous campaigns. Closely-watched exit polls showed Yushchenko leading with 53 percent of the vote. However, the government-controlled election commission announced that Yanukovych won with 49.5 percent over Yushchenko's 46.9 percent.

Yushchenko's outraged supporters promptly charged that the official results had been rigged. When overwhelming evidence supported this accusation, protestors began to gather in late November, 2004 in the Maiden, Kyiv's large Independence Square. The spontaneous demonstrations became known as the Orange Revolution after Yushchenko's official campaign color. On one occasion over 500,000

Ukrainian citizens gathered in the Maiden to demand a new election and the end of political corruption.

The outpouring of peaceful protests worked. The Ukrainian Constitutional Court annulled the election results as fraudulent and ordered a new vote on December 26, 2004. As expected, Yushchenko won with 52 percent of the vote.

HOPE AND DISILLUSIONMENT, 2005 – 2010

The Orange Revolution raised great hopes for change. In his victory speech, Yushchenko reinforced this expectation when he proudly declared, "We are free. The old era is over. We are a new country now."

Yushchenko's supporters expected their new president to revive Ukraine's economy, reduce corruption, and bring the nation closer to the European Union. Faced with these difficult challenges, Yushchenko achieved mixed results. Although Ukraine's GNP doubled, rampant corruption continued. At the same time, a bitter power struggle with Prime Minister Yulia Tymoshenko created a political stalemate that prevented the enactment of needed reforms. As the initial spirit of hope faded, disillusioned Ukrainians increasingly felt their country was neither a fair place to work or an honest place to do business.

The widespread disillusionment with the Yushchenko presidency enabled Viktor Yanukovych to stage a remarkable political comeback. Aided by a team of skilled political consultants, Yanukovych presented himself as a pragmatic leader who would stress moderate domestic and international policies. Five years after he failed to steal the 2004 election, Yanukovych won a convincing victory in a free and fair election.

POWER AND CORRUPTION

Yanukovych quickly ignored his campaign promises. Although elected by a slim majority, he moved decisively to consolidate power and eliminate political rivals. Yanukovych used million-dollar bribes to help "persuade" members of Parliament to change laws that constrained him. He further bolstered his power by bringing the police, army, and security services under his firm control.

Having achieved unfettered control over the executive branch, Yanukovych moved to enrich himself and his allies. In less than 4 years, he and a small group of associates known as "The Family" used lucrative insider deals, overpriced construction projects, and cheap loans from state-owned banks to loot as much as $100 billion. For example, Yanukovych's son worked as a dentist while amassing a fortune of over $500 million.

MEZHYHIRYA, A "DICTATORSHIP THEME PARK"

Yanukovych was not content to live in the presidential residence in Kyiv. Instead, he erased the memories of his impoverished childhood by building a $2.5 billion private estate on a 345 acre hillside overlooking the Dnipro River.

Known as Mezhyhirya, Yanukovych's "villa" provided a concrete symbol of his opulent taste and disregard for the living conditions of average Ukrainians. Described by one commentator as a "dictatorship theme park," Mezhyhirya featured a vast, multi-leveled home constructed with the finest wood and polished marble floors. Yanukovych decorated rooms with expensive silver chandeliers, rare pianos, and valuable works of art. He impressed his guests by inviting them to enjoy boxing matches in a private gym, watch James Bond movies in a lavish movie theater, and admire his collection of over 70 vintage cars.

"WE HAVE HAD OUR FUTURE TAKEN FROM US"

Although hopelessly corrupt, Yanukovych seemed firmly in control. However, a massive popular uprising in late 2013 caught him and the world by surprise. During his presidency, Yanukovych negotiated an Associate Agreement with the European Union. The Ukrainian public supported the agreement, believing its free-trade provisions would create new economic opportunities.

On November 21, 2013, just one week before a scheduled signing ceremony, Yanukovych abruptly suspended talks with the European Union. Pressured by Russian President Vladimir Putin, he announced the beginning of talks to provide closer economic ties with a Russian-led Customs Union.

The sudden change of course dashed widespread hopes for a better life. A prominent Ukrainian writer expressed the public mood of frustration and outrage when he wrote, "Once again, we have had our future taken from us.

THE REVOLUTION OF DIGNITY

Angry Ukrainians were unwilling to passively allow the Yanukovych government to steal their future. On November 21, 2013, demonstrators gathered on the Maiden in downtown Kyiv. Encouraged by social media, their numbers steadily rose.

The protests began as a response to the suspension of talks to sign an Associate Agreement with the European Union. This issue-specific protest might have gradually faded. However, Yanukovych overreacted by ordering riot police to use batons and stun grenades to disperse the crowds gathered on the Maiden. The government's excessive use of force energized the demonstrators and galvanized widespread public support. The police brutality thus transformed the demonstrators into a popular Revolution of Dignity in which Ukrainians demanded an end to government corruption and a return to the rule of law.

The growing Revolution of Dignity quickly turned into a contest over the future of the Yanukovych regime. Aware of the growing threat to his power, Yanukovych ordered his security forces to use live ammunition and flash grenades to suppress the crowds gathered in downtown Kyiv. The escalating violence claimed the lives of over 100 protesters.

The loss of life outraged Ukrainians. Shouts of "It's time!" and "Down with the criminal gang!" filled the streets in cities across the country. Yanukovych now realized that his days in power were numbered. On February 22, 2014, he secretly fled to Russia.

"GLORY TO UKRAINE"

When he wrote the Ukrainian Declaration of Independence, Levko Lukianenko dreamed that Ukraine would become a prosperous, independent, and democratic country. Yanukovych's sudden ouster seemed to signal that his vision would become a reality. Jubilant Ukrainians shouted, "Glory to Ukraine" and hoped for the beginning of a dramatic new chapter in their history. But in Moscow, Russian President Vladimir Putin had a very different view of Ukraine's future.

CHAPTER 7

THE EMPIRE STRIKES BACK, 2014 – 2019

CHAPTER 7
THE EMPIRE STRIKES BACK, 2014 - 2019

The Revolution of Dignity appeared to open a new and peaceful chapter in Ukrainian history. While the West applauded the fall of the corrupt Yanukovych regime, Russian President Vladimir Putin viewed the unexpected event with alarm.

Putin felt that he had to undertake a decisive response. On February 22, 2014, he convened an all-night meeting of his senior security officials to consider the possibility of seizing control of the Crimean Peninsula. Putin's defense minister and other advisers unanimously opposed the idea. They argued that the plan risked triggering a punitive wave of costly Western economic sanctions and a potentially bloody Ukrainian military response.

Their arguments did not persuade Putin. Shortly before sunrise, he announced his decision. Putin overruled the group and confidently concluded, "We are forced to begin work to bring Crimea into Russia."

Putin is recognized as a careful and calculating strategist. Faced with the possible loss of Russian influence in Kyiv, why did he turn his attention to Crimea? What did he mean by the phrase "bring Crimea into Russia?" What did he hope to gain?

CRIMEA - LOCATION AND IMPORTANCE

As you can see in the map on page XII, Crimea is a peninsula located along the northern coast of the Black Sea. With an area of 10,425 square miles, it is almost the same size as Massachusetts. Its pleasing combination of scenic beaches, nearby mountains, and a mild subtropical climate, have made Crimea a popular destination for Russian tourists.

Crimea made a dramatic appearance in American history when British Prime Minister Winston Churchill, American President Franklin D.

Roosevelt, and Soviet leader Joseph Stalin met in early February 1945 at the resort city of Yalta. Known as the "Big Three," the Allied leaders gathered to celebrate the impending defeat of Nazi Germany and negotiate the fate of Eastern Europe.

While Crimea makes a brief appearance in American history, it occupies a prominent place in Russian history. In 1783, Catherine the Great seized control of Crimea from the Ottoman Empire. Within a short time, the peninsula's strategic port of Sevastopol became the headquarters of the Russian Black Sea Fleet. During World War II, Sevastopol became the site of an intense and pivotal battle between the Soviet Red Army and Nazi Germany. Russian residents still revere Sevastopol as holy ground where "every cobblestone is covered in the blood of our fathers and grandfathers."

In 1954, Soviet Premier Nikita Khrushchev surprised Crimean residents when he transferred the peninsula from Russian to Ukrainian jurisdiction. Intended to celebrate the "great and indissoluble friendship" of the Russian and Ukrainian people, the act seemed a meaningless bureaucratic transfer of territory. As noted by an American diplomat in Kyiv, "For Khrushchev this was like moving a ruble from his right pocket to his left pocket. Given the centralized makeup of the Soviet Union, it didn't make much difference."

Crimea remained a part of Ukraine following the dissolution of the Soviet Union in 1991. As long as pro-Russian governments held power in Kyiv, the peninsula and its strategic port of Sevastopol remained an uncontested part of Ukraine. But that changed when the fall of the Yanukovych government appeared to foreshadow the election of a new, pro-Western Ukrainian government.

"I MADE A DECISION"

Putin repeatedly and forcefully insisted that Crimea "has always been an inseparable part of Russia." He viewed Khrushchev's incorporation of Crimea into Ukraine as an "outrageous historical injustice." As the self-proclaimed guardian of the Russian people, Putin believed he had a responsibility to protect ethnic Russians living in Crimea.

Ethnic Russians constituted a majority of Crimea's population. Public opinion polls in Crimea and Russia reported strong support for restoring Crimea to the Russian Federation. Putin calculated that a successful annexation would rally public support while diverting attention from pressing economic problems.

The political chaos unleashed by Yanukovych's sudden fall from power created weakness and indecision in Kyiv. Putin recognized that the leaders of Ukraine's provisional government lacked the ability to undertake decisive actions. Kyiv's vulnerability created an opportunity for Putin to put into motion a carefully prepared contingency plan to annex Crimea. From his point of view, the benefits of seizing Crimea far outweighed the risks. The time had come to act: "We saw what was happening in Kyiv and I made a decision."

THE "LITTLE GREEN MEN"

A series of carefully coordinated events swiftly followed Putin's decision. On February 27, 2014, 60 heavily-armed men seized the Crimean Parliament and then raised a Russian flag above the building. The next day, soldiers wearing unmarked green uniforms captured police stations, airports, and key transportation intersections. Known as "little green men," the troops soon gained control over the entire Crimean peninsula.

Putin and his Foreign Minister Sergei Lavrov issued public statements assuring the international community that the armed soldiers were local Crimean defense units. But their deliberate use of disinformation could not mask the reality of what was happening – Russia was in fact redrawing the recognized border of a sovereign European nation.

"KRYM NASH – CRIMEA IS OURS!"

Putin easily brushed aside international criticism of Russia's unilateral action. He insisted that Moscow had an obligation to protect ethnic Russians living in Crimea from the "far-right extremists" who overthrew the Yanukovych government. Putin offered proof of the popular support for his intervention by pointing to a referendum conducted on March 16, 2014 in which over 97 percent of Crimean voters supported joining the Russian Federation.

Disputed by Ukraine and the West, the referendum nonetheless provided a legal pretext for the Kremlin's immediate annexation of Crimea. On March 18th, Putin formally signed a treaty of accession bringing Crimea into the Russian Federation. Speaking to hundreds of officials in the Kremlin's ornate St. George Hall, Putin received thunderous applause when he declared, "Crimea has always been an integral part of Russia in the hearts and minds of people." The cheering audience repeatedly signaled their overwhelming approval by shouting, "Krym Nash – Crimea is ours!"

"THERE IS NOTHING TO FEAR"

Held from February 7-23rd in Sochi, Russia, the Winter Olympics coincided with the climatic days of the ongoing Ukrainian Revolution of Dignity. Putin concluded the Games by proudly boasting, "The Games opened the door not only to Russia, but also to the Russian soul, to the hearts of our people. Others could look and see that there is nothing to fear, that we are open for cooperation." Putin launched the takeover of Crimea less than one week later. His brazen military aggression belied the pledge that "there is nothing to fear."

Stunned world leaders condemned Russia's violation of the international rules-based order. Known as the Group of Eight (G8), leaders of the world's foremost economic powers had planned to hold their annual summit meeting at a specially built luxury hotel in Sochi. Instead, they canceled the meeting and removed Russia from the G8. Although this and other economic sanctions may have stung Putin's pride, they did not persuade him to relinquish Russia's firm control over Crimea.

"I TOOK RESPONSIBILITY FOR EVERYTHING"

The swift and nearly bloodless annexation of Crimea boosted Putin's confidence in his own judgment. He proudly boasted, "I took responsibility for everything. I will be gone sooner or later, but Crimea will have been returned to Russia forever."

The successful seizure of the Crimean Peninsula had important consequences. The West's limited sanctions had little impact on the Russian economy thus reducing their effectiveness as a deterrent. The abysmal performance of the Ukrainian military further convinced Putin that Ukraine was an artificial nation that would not defend itself. And finally, the seizure of Crimea emboldened Putin to disregard cautious advisors and trust his own seemingly infallible judgment. With his personal popularity inside Russia soaring to new heights, Putin came to see himself as part of a select group of legendary Russian leaders led by his hero Peter the Great.

THE DONBAS

Putin now turned his attention to a region in southeastern Ukraine known as the Donbas. As you can see on the map on page XIII, the Donbas is divided into the Luhansk and Donetsk provinces.

The Donbas's economic development began with the discovery of the region's vast coal resources. During the late 1800s, railroads connected the coal mines to nearby iron ore deposits. This transportation link promoted the growth of a thriving steel industry.

Both the Nazis and Soviets coveted the Donbas as a key economic prize. The region began to recover from fierce battles when a post-World War II migration of Soviet workers revitalized the region and transformed its cities into enclaves of Russian culture. Although the Donbas became a part of Ukraine, a significant portion of its population retained linguistic, cultural, and family ties with Russia.

The Donbas's status as an industrial powerhouse steadily declined during the 1990s and 2000s. Living standards fell as the region's outdated coal and steel industries could no longer compete with global safety standards. For example, Ukraine's coal mines had the dubious distinction of recording the second-highest accident rate in the world. Only China recorded a higher death rate.

A "FROZEN CONFLICT"

Ukrainian activists believed the Revolution of Dignity had transformed Ukraine into a truly independent modern country. One proud resident of Lviv insisted, "That was when social consciousness changed, when the Soviet Union inside us died." Although ties to the Soviet Union may have withered in central and western Ukraine, they remained strong in the Donbas. While many Ukrainian cities removed statues dedicated to Lenin, in the Donbas these monuments remained as visible symbols of attachment to Soviet history and ideology.

A combination of pro-Russian sentiment, economic stagnation, and distrust of the corrupt government in Kyiv made the Donbas fertile ground for a separatist movement. Emboldened by support from Putin, armed men seized control of government buildings throughout the Donbas. In April 2014, pro-Russian separatists declared the formation of People's Republics in both Luhansk and Donetsk.

The Ukrainian government refused to acknowledge the legitimacy of the two breakaway republics. Kyiv soon launched a successful military counter-offensive. By late August 2014, Ukrainian forces significantly rolled back territory held by pro-Russian forces.

Putin responded to the Ukrainian success by ordering regular units of the Russian army to cross the border. Although Ukraine could defeat the separatists, its army could not repel the larger and better-equipped

Russian forces. Both armies built extensive networks of trenches, bunkers, and tunnels that resembled the Western Front during World War I. The trench warfare led to what became widely described as a "frozen conflict" that claimed the lives of thousands of soldiers and civilians.

"UKRAINE HAS NOT YET PERISHED"

Undaunted by the escalating conflict in the Donbas, Ukraine held a presidential election on May 25, 2014. Voters elected Petro Poroshenko, a wealthy oligarch and experienced politician. Known as the "Chocolate King," Poroshenko owned a large confectionary company that manufactured over 200 kinds of chocolate and other candies. His business empire also included car and bus factories, a shipyard, and a television channel.

Poroshenko experienced moderate successes in tackling Ukraine's pressing problems. He began the process of integration with the European Union by signing the Associate Agreement Yanukovych had backed out of. However, he was unable to negotiate an end to the war in the Donbas.

Poroshenko vowed to reduce the corrupt business practices that had long undermined Ukraine's economy and contributed to the popular outrage that led to Yanukovych's ouster. Although he promised transparency, a trove of confidential documents from a Panama-based law firm revealed that Poroshenko had secretly moved assets he promised to sell into an offshore holding company in the British Virgin Islands.

The scandal shook public confidence in Poroshenko. Widespread disillusionment created an opportunity for Volodymyr Zelensky, a charismatic, anti-establishment political newcomer to enter the political arena. Unlike the career politicians and oligarchs who had previously governed Ukraine, Zelensky was a popular television and movie actor who understood how to use social media. Zelensky's novel rise to power began when he starred in a popular televised drama called Servant of the People. Zelensky played a history teacher whose passionate lesson against corruption went viral and catapulted him to the presidency.

Fiction became reality when Zelensky formed his own real-life Servant of the People political party. Untarnished by political or economic corruption, he won a landslide victory over Poroshenko. Zelensky took office on May 20, 2019. He offered hope to an embattled but resilient nation that continued to believe in the opening words of its stirring national anthem: "Ukraine has not yet perished."

CHAPTER 8
"DON'T TRUST PUTIN"

CHAPTER 8
"DON'T TRUST PUTIN"

No one knew what to expect as Ukrainian President Volodymyr Zelensky entered the Élysée Palace in Paris to attend a summit meeting on December 9, 2019, with Russian President Vladimir Putin. In office for just six months, the inexperienced former television sitcom star arrived in a modest gray Renault minivan. In contrast, the calculating former KGB officer and seasoned ruler for nearly two decades arrived in an Aurus, a massive Russian-made armored limousine.

French President Emmanuel Macron and German Chancellor Angela Merkel served as co-hosts for the summit. The talks focused on resolving the ongoing conflict in a region of southeastern Ukraine known as the Donbas. Since it began in 2014, the grinding struggle between Ukrainian and separatist forces had claimed the lives of more than 13,000 combatants and civilians.

The face-to-face talks did produce modest progress. Zelensky and Putin agreed to reduce tensions by exchanging prisoners and calling for a cease-fire. However, major obstacles still remained. Putin's price for a settlement included greater autonomy for the breakaway republics of Luhansk and Donetsk. In addition, Putin demanded a binding guarantee that Ukraine would not join the North Atlantic Treaty Organization (NATO). Zelensky rejected both demands as unacceptable infringements on Ukraine's status as an independent sovereign nation.

In a press conference following the summit, Zelensky admitted that several unsettled issues remained. However, he optimistically predicted that the summit marked "a big step toward peace." Zelensky's hopeful forecast proved to be tragically wrong Prior to the summit, his predecessor Petro Poroshenko issued this blunt advice: "Don't trust Putin. Never. At all. Putin manipulates everything: content, facts, numbers, maps, emotions.

He hates Ukraine and Ukrainians." The unfolding events following the Paris summit would more than justify Poroshenko's warning.

THE CREATION OF NATO

From Putin's point of view, his summit meeting with Zelensky represented a small brush stroke in a much larger geopolitical canvas. Putin's long-range strategic goals included returning Ukraine to Russia's sphere of influence, restoring Russia's status as a respected great power, and weakening the NATO alliance.

NATO's origins stretched back to the beginning of the Cold War. The United States and the Soviet Union emerged from World War II as the world's foremost military superpowers. Keenly aware of America's military strength, Soviet leader Joseph Stalin wanted a buffer region of friendly communist countries along Russia's western border. Stalin's determination to dominate Eastern Europe quickly became a reality as he began to install pro-Soviet regimes throughout the region. In a speech delivered on March 6, 1947 at Westminster College in Fulton, Missouri, Winston Churchill warned, "An Iron Curtain has descended across the Continent."

Alarmed by Churchill's grim warning, the Truman administration searched for a new foreign policy to meet the Soviet challenge. George Kennan, a leading expert on Russian history, published an influential essay in which he argued that animosity was deeply rooted in Russia's long-standing mistrust of the West. He pointed out that Russian leaders, from the country's first Tsar Ivan the Terrible to Stalin, viewed the outside world with suspicion, envy, and hostility. Given this history of antagonism, Kennan recommended that the United States should adopt a policy of vigilant containment to prevent Soviet expansion.

The Truman administration agreed with Kennan's analysis and recommendation. In 1949, the United States joined Canada and ten Western European countries to form the North Atlantic Treaty Organization (NATO). The alliance members pledged to work together to preserve regional stability. Although the pact bound its members to settle international disputes by peaceful means, Article 5 stated that "the Parties agree that an armed attack against one or more of them in Europe or North America shall be considered an attack against them all." This unequivocal statement of collective security tied American military power to the defense of each NATO member.

THE DECISION TO ENLARGE NATO

Greece, Turkey, and West Germany joined NATO in the early 1950s. These additions increased NATO's collective power and helped the alliance fulfill its mission of deterring Soviet expansion.

The collapse of the Soviet Union in 1991 forced NATO to adjust to the end of the Cold War. Confronted with a new geopolitical reality, NATO modified its mission from containing the Soviet Union to promoting a "Europe whole, free, and at peace." Led by Lech Walesa in Poland and Vaclav Havel in the Czech Republic, a new generation of democratically elected Eastern European leaders urged NATO to include countries that had once been Soviet satellites. They stressed that the addition of Poland, the Czech Republic, and Hungary would erase the arbitrary line Stalin drew through Europe.

The controversial decision to enlarge NATO sparked a heated debate. George Kennan published a widely read essay in the New York Times forcefully stating that expanding NATO would be "a fateful error" because it would "inflame the nationalistic, anti-Western and militaristic tendencies in Russian opinion." Other influential critics reminded American officials that Russian leaders had grown up learning to fear and oppose NATO. Needlessly expanding the alliance would damage American efforts to transform Russia from a Cold War enemy to a post-Cold War partner.

Supporters of NATO expansion countered by reminding critics that European political and military realities required a strong alliance. Secretary of State Madeleine Albright recounted the frightening story of how her family fled to the United States from communist-controlled Czechoslovakia. Albright argued that NATO represented a necessary hedge against the risk of a more belligerent Russia. She underscored this point when she told the Senate Armed Services Committee, "On the off-chance that in fact Russia doesn't work out the way we are hoping it will … NATO is there."

The perceived need to protect Eastern Europe's new democracies from a possible future Russian threat prevailed. Albright and her supporters hailed the enlargement of NATO as a victory for freedom and democracy. On March 12, 1999, Albright stood with the foreign ministers of Poland, Hungary, and the Czech Republic in the auditorium of the Truman Presidential Library in Independence, Missouri, and formally welcomed these three countries into the NATO alliance.

PUTIN AND NATO

Vladimir Putin became President of Russia in 2000. He did not hail NATO's expansion as a victory for freedom and democracy in Europe. Instead, he perceived NATO as Russia's "main opponent." Putin's growing sense of alarm became more pronounced in 2004 when NATO once again expanded its membership by adding Bulgaria, Romania, Slovakia, Slovenia, and the three Baltic states of Estonia, Lithuania, and Latvia. The inclusion of the Baltic states especially incensed Putin because they had been part of the Soviet Union.

Putin viewed NATO's continued expansion as a clear threat to Russia's national security. The rift between Russia and the West burst into public view at the Munich Security Conference in 2007. Putin shocked an audience of Western diplomats and political leaders by angrily declaring, "I think it is obvious that NATO expansion does not have any relation with ensuring security in Europe. On the contrary, it represents a serious provocation that reduces the level of mutual trust." He then pointedly asked, "Against whom is this expansion intended?"

Putin's bellicose speech signaled the end of qualified optimism for broader Western cooperation with Russia. Putin soon proclaimed his intention to restore Russia's status as a respected and feared great power. His view of Russian greatness did not mean strengthening democratic institutions and the rule of law. Instead, he began to systematically dismantle Russia's fledgling democracy by exercising greater control over media outlets, suppressing rival political parties, and launching a massive program to rebuild the Russian military.

PUTIN AND UKRAINE

Ukraine remained the largest unaligned nation located between Russia and NATO countries. As a result, it occupied a particularly important place in Putin's geopolitical thinking. Like previous Russian and Soviet leaders, Putin accepted the concept that Russia must maintain a buffer or strategic depth between its heartland and the powerful European adversaries to the west.

Ukraine's size, natural resources, and location made it a geopolitical prize. In addition, Putin insisted that Ukraine and Russia were bound together by close cultural, religious, and linguistic ties. He understood and agreed with U.S. National Security Advisor Zbigniew Brezezinski's observation that, "Without Ukraine, Russia ceases to be an empire, but with Ukraine suborned [unlawfully bribed or induced] and then subordinated, Russia automatically becomes an empire."

Putin tried and repeatedly failed to restore Ukraine to a subordinate place in Russia's sphere of influence. However, the Orange Revolution in 2004 and the Revolution of Dignity in 2014 both derailed his efforts to install pro-Russian governments. Instead, Ukraine sought to forge its own path as a sovereign state.

Putin became increasingly alarmed as the Zelensky government steadily moved away from Russian influence and domination. For example, the United States and some NATO allies began a multi-year program to train and equip Ukraine's armed forces. From Putin's point of view, Ukraine was rapidly becoming a de facto member of NATO.

Putin believed he could not allow Ukraine to live in peace and slip out of Russia's sphere of influence. A modern democratic Ukraine would inevitably undermine his autocratic regime. During his years as a KGB agent stationed in Dresden, Putin witnessed how West Germany's economic success eroded public confidence in the East German communist regime. He keenly understood that a prosperous Ukraine would inevitably highlight Russia's shortcomings. Putin and his inner circle of oligarchs could not accept a future in which political opponents were free to organize opposition parties, reporters were free to write critical articles, and voters were free to choose independent leaders.

ESCALATION AND RISING TENSIONS

Acutely aware of both Ukraine's geopolitical importance and its potential to undermine his authoritarian rule, Putin began to escalate regional tensions. During the spring of 2021, he positioned thousands of Russian troops around Ukraine's eastern border. Officials in Moscow publicly claimed the soldiers were participating in planned military exercises.

Russia's military maneuvers did not end. Instead, they continued to escalate during the fall and winter months. By late December 2021, a massive force of almost 200,000 Russian soldiers conducted increasingly ominous war games on Ukraine's northern, eastern, and southern borders.

Putin's provocative display of force alarmed American military and intelligence officials. Satellite images and intercepted high-level Russian communications strongly pointed to the imminent threat of an all-out Russian invasion of Ukraine. But European skeptics remained unconvinced. They pointed out that Americans had erroneously claimed that Iraq had weapons of mass destruction. They also questioned America's credibility after its deeply flawed overestimation of the Afghan government's ability to resist the Taliban.

Given these concerns, few leaders in Europe or Ukraine believed Putin intended to begin a major war. Aware of the Russian dictator's well-deserved reputation as a master of crisis diplomacy, most observers assumed Putin was using the military buildup to intimidate Ukraine and weaken the Zelensky government.

"AN EXCHANGE OF HOT AIR"

As tension escalated, Western leaders attempted to avert an armed conflict by engaging Putin in a series of high-stakes negotiations. President Biden sent William Burns, his director of the Central Intelligence Agency (CIA), to Moscow to convey America's "serious concerns" about the growing crisis. Biden further emphasized America's resolve when he warned Putin that the West would impose severe sanctions on the Russian economy.

The threat of crippling sanctions did not deter Putin. He responded by insisting that Ukraine was a "made-up country" that was in reality a cultural and historical part of Russia. In a blatant attempt to weaken NATO, Putin demanded that the alliance withdraw all multinational forces from its Eastern European members and agree to close its door to Ukraine and other former Soviet republics.

The standoff between Putin's unacceptable demands and the West's threat of unprecedented sanctions continued into February 2022. French President Emmanuel Macron visited Moscow in a last-ditch attempt to find a path to a peaceful settlement. His meeting inside the Kremlin attracted global attention. Forced to sit at the end of a 20-foot-long table from the socially isolating Russian dictator, Macron patiently listened to Putin's long list of grievances and demands. He returned to Paris pessimistically warning that chances for peace were irrevocably fading.

The deadlocked talks with Putin appeared to leave no diplomatic solution. Lila Shevtsova, a respected authority on Putin, concluded that the Western leaders had "engaged in an exchange of hot air." As Ukraine's destiny hung precariously in the balance, Petro Poroshenko's warning in 2019 seemed ominously prescient: "Don't trust Putin. Never. At all."

CHAPTER 9
THE BATTLE FOR KYIV

CHAPTER 9
THE BATTLE FOR KYIV

What does Putin want? During the first weeks of 2022, this urgent question dominated global headlines and national security meetings in capitals throughout the Western world. Putin abruptly ended speculation when he delivered a surprise early morning address broadcasted by Russian state television on February 24, 2022.

Seated at a desk in the Kremlin, Putin began his 30-minute speech by listing long-held grievances against NATO expansion and American arrogance. He then announced a "special military operation" to "demilitarize and denazify" Ukraine. In a menacing address filled with threats, Putin warned that any "outside forces" attempting to aid Ukraine would confront "consequences of the sort that you have not faced in your history."

Putin's unprovoked invasion of Ukraine marked the beginning of the largest military operation in Europe since the end of World War II. It thus ended a golden age of peace and prosperity that historians of international relations call the "Long Peace." Europe now entered a new and much more dangerous period of history.

PUTIN'S STRATEGIC CALCULUS

Within minutes of Putin's speech, long columns of Russian tanks invaded Ukraine from the north, south, and east. At the same time, precision guided missiles pounded Ukrainian air defenses, radar batteries, and ammunition depots. This was not a limited strike in the Donbas that many officials had predicted. Instead, the inconceivable was happening – Putin was launching a full-scale invasion of Ukraine.

The invasion began a new era in Putin's long-standing attempt to control events in Ukraine. Thwarted by Ukraine's desire for closer ties with the West, he unleashed a seemingly invincible military force to seize control of the entire country. Putin turned to this ruthless strategy because he saw a window of opportunity in which the rewards of subduing Ukraine seemed to far outweigh the risks.

Putin's strategic calculus began with the assumption that Russia's superior military forces would achieve a certain and swift victory by crushing Ukraine's outnumbered defenders and then seizing Kyiv. Assassination squads would capture or kill President Zelensky and other Ukrainian officials. The Kremlin would then fill the power vacuum by installing a puppet government tied to its masters in Moscow. Putin's intelligence agencies assured him that the Ukrainians would welcome their Russian "liberators" and embrace their new government.

Putin understood that outraged Western leaders would loudly protest the invasion. However, he calculated that Russia's nuclear arsenal would deter NATO from becoming militarily involved inside Ukraine. Although he expected sanctions, warnings about crippling economic penalties did not deter Putin. He shrewdly recognized that the economies of Germany, France, Italy, and other European countries were heavily dependent upon imported Russian oil and gas. And finally, Putin believed America's humiliating withdrawal from Afghanistan would discourage President Biden from becoming deeply involved in a new war.

Putin did not anticipate any meaningful domestic opposition to the invasion. His massive security forces stood ready to stifle any protests. At the same time, the Kremlin's well-oiled propaganda machine would mobilize popular support for the invasion.

Confident in his own strength and sensing weakness in America and NATO, Putin concluded that he had far more to gain than to lose. The successful conquest of Ukraine would reverse historic wrongs and establish his legacy as one of Russia's greatest rulers.

"I NEED AMMUNITION, NOT A RIDE"

President Zelensky's private phone suddenly rang at 4:15 A.M. on February 24th. His Interior Minister wasted no time before delivering an urgent message: "It has started." Briefly startled, Zelensky asked, "What exactly?" He then learned that Putin had ordered a full-scale invasion that was raining "terrible blows" on Ukrainian forces while simultaneously heading directly toward Kyiv.

Within the next hours, more alarming news continued to inundate Zelensky. European leaders and Western military experts all warned that the outnumbered Ukrainian forces could not resist Russia's overwhelming military power. Concerned for his personal safety, worried American officials offered to evacuate Zelensky and his family to a safe refuge in western Ukraine or in Poland.

Now located in a bomb shelter deep beneath Kyiv's government quarter, Zelensky had to make a fateful decision. Putin confidently expected the young and untested leader to panic and flee. He recalled that in 2014, Ukraine's pro-Russian president Viktor Yanukovych fled during the Revolution of Dignity. And just a few months before in August 2021, the United States-supported Ashraf Ghani, President of Afghanistan, fled his country as the Taliban surrounded Kabul.

Unlike these cowardly leaders, Zelensky did not vacillate or flee. He bluntly informed his close advisors that he would not leave Kyiv. In a display of unwavering resolve, Zelensky rejected the American offer by responding, "The fight is here; I need ammunition, not a ride."

Zelensky backed up his brave words with defiant actions. On February 25th he left his bomb shelter and stood in front of a widely recognized public building. Zelensky calmly but firmly told a nationwide audience, "We are all here. Our troops are here ..We are defending the independence of our country…Glory to Ukraine."

Zelensky's courage and conviction rallied the Ukrainian people by providing them with a clear moral purpose. They would not allow Putin to erase Ukraine's national identity. Determined to live as free men and women, Ukrainians would defend their homeland and the future liberty of their children.

"THIS IS OUR CITY"

Putin ignored Zelensky's vow to resist the Russian invasion. He confidently believed that the Ukrainian people would welcome Russian soldiers as liberators from a corrupt and unpopular government. Anticipating an easy victory and a warm welcome, many Russian troops packed brightly-colored dress uniforms they expected to wear during a triumphant march through downtown Kyiv.

Kyiv's defiant citizens did not prepare a welcoming parade. Within a short time, their initial shock gave way to a fierce resolve to defend their beleaguered city. While air-raid sirens pierced the skies and massive explosions rocked the city, men and women constructed a network of barricades to block both major highways and the famed cobblestone streets in Kyiv's old town.

Kyiv's citizens did more than man barricades; they also armed themselves. Government trucks loaded with rifles distributed weapons to people of all ages. A picture of Kira Rudnik, a 36-year-old member of the Ukrainian Parliament, armed with an automatic rifle captured global headlines. Rudnik voiced her city's defiant mood when she told a CNN reporter: "I planned to plant tulips and daffodils in my backyard today. Instead, I learn to fire arms and get ready for the next night of attack on Kyiv. This is our city, our land, and our soil. We will fight for it."

"WE WILL NOT FIGHT THE THIRD WORLD WAR IN UKRAINE"

Putin's brutal invasion of Ukraine did not go as planned. Instead of erasing Ukraine's national identity, his tanks and missiles forged a unified national response. Across Ukraine, students who should have been carrying books armed themselves with assault rifles. At the same time, pictures of bombed apartment buildings, ruined schools, and terrified children galvanized public support in free countries across the world.

Russia's unprovoked attack on a sovereign nation confronted NATO with a difficult dilemma. Ukraine is not a member of NATO and thus not entitled to military protection from alliance members, yet Ukraine's survival as an independent country is in NATO's interest. The fall of Ukraine would undermine NATO's credibility and invite further Russian aggression. How could the NATO countries stand idly by and watch the Russian war machine conquer a people who desired to live as free men and women in a democratic country?

President Biden attempted to walk a fine line between aiding Ukraine and avoiding a dangerous escalation that could turn a regional war into a global conflict between nuclear-armed countries. Pressed on his decision to not use American air power to enforce a no-fly zone over Ukraine, President Biden insisted, "That's called World War III...We will not fight the third world war in Ukraine."

Unwilling to provoke a direct military confrontation with Russia, the United States and its NATO allies nonetheless imposed a range of sanctions designed to isolate and cripple the Russian economy. At the same time, America and Great Britain supplied the Ukrainian army with lethal anti-aircraft and anti-tank weapons. And finally, President Biden strongly warned Moscow that the United States would defend "every inch of territory of NATO countries with the full force of our collective power."

"I THINK KYIV FALLS IN JUST A FEW DAYS"

The Russian onslaught on Kyiv began with a lightning assault by attack helicopters and elite paratroopers on the Antonov Airport. Located just six miles from the outskirts of the capital, the cargo airport would then serve as a base for airlifting more troops and equipment to directly threaten Kyiv. Confident Russian commanders believed that a quick strike on the airport would paralyze the Ukrainian military and demoralize the Zelensky government.

While the Russians attacked the Antonov Airport, powerful armored columns poured across the border into Ukraine. With a 10-to-1 advantage in manpower and a 20-to-1 advantage in artillery, Putin's war machine appeared to be invincible. In Washington, a senior intelligence officer predicted that the outnumbered and outgunned Ukrainian forces would soon collapse: "I think Kyiv falls in just a few days. This isn't going to last long."

Few questioned the intelligence officer's pessimistic forecast. During the early days of the invasion, each night felt darker than the last. Satellite images of a massive 40-mile-long armored column heading inexorably toward Kyiv added to the growing sense of tension. Across the world, anxious Ukrainian supporters woke up each morning to check the news headlines, wondering if Kyiv was still resisting and if Zelensky was still alive.

"WE ARE LIKE A HIVE OF BEES"

Ukraine's fate hung in the balance as the Russian tanks pressed toward Kyiv. Despite facing enormous odds, a combination of resourceful Ukrainian soldiers and valiant citizen volunteers found the courage and motivation to fight rather than flee. "We are like a hive of bees," boasted one citizen-soldier. "One bee is nothing, but a thousand can defeat a big force."

The volunteer "bees" and professional Ukrainian soldiers confused and startled the Russian invaders. For example, Russian strategy called for their elite units to capture the strategic Antonov Airport, located just 20 miles from the center of Kyiv. But fierce resistance heavily damaged the airport's runways and prevented it from serving as a functional base for Russian troops.

"WELCOME TO HELL!"

Frustrated by the failure of their plan to quickly seize Kyiv, Russian commanders pushed southward along both sides of the Dnipro River. But they continued to underestimate the Ukrainian army's unwavering will to fight. Ukrainian defenders welcomed the Russian invaders by spray painting overpasses and highway signs with a grim warning – "Welcome to Hell!"

The Ukrainians' message was not a bluff. Their defense forces stymied the Russian advance by destroying roads, blowing up bridges, and even deliberately opening dams to create floods. The region's dense forests, narrow roads, and winding rivers all promoted guerilla tactics. Moving stealthily at night, small groups of Ukrainian soldiers successfully ambushed unsuspecting Russian units.

Although Ukrainian soldiers had a shortage of heavy artillery and tanks, they did possess thousands of portable anti-tank weapons called Javelins supplied by the U.S. The weapon's precision-guided warhead can destroy modern tanks by striking them from above where their armor is thinnest. The Javelin's fire-and-forget design uses automatic infrared guidance that allows soldiers to seek cover immediately after launching it. The Javelin thus provided a relatively low-cost but lethal weapon that revolutionized the battlefield by destroying hundreds of Russian tanks and armored personnel carriers.

Javelins were not the only sophisticated weapon in the Ukrainian arsenal. They also successfully used Starlink, a satellite communication system owned and operated by Elon Musk's SpaceX company. Thousands of Starlink terminals enabled Ukrainians to prevent Russian jammers from cutting them off from the internet. As a result, front line soldiers and civilians in besieged cities could communicate with their families and friends. The terminals also enabled President Zelensky to provide daily updates to the Ukrainian people and to hold Zoom calls with global leaders.

"WE HELD THEM BACK!"

Putin's invading forces failed to reach Kyiv. The Ukrainians successfully repelled the Russian advance at key strategic points on the outskirts of the city. A Ukrainian company commander proudly reported, "We held them back!"

Ukrainian forces did more than hold their ground. In late March they mounted a determined counterattack that inflicted heavy losses on the Russians. Within days battered Russian units began to retreat from northern Ukraine. On March 29th, a Kremlin spokesman officially confirmed Moscow's decision to withdraw when he issued a statement declaring the Kremlin's intention to "drastically reduce military activity in the direction of Kyiv." But this decision did not end the war. Putin now indicated that Russian forces would regroup and then shift their resources to "liberate" the Donbas region in the east.

The victorious battle to save Kyiv protected Ukraine's independence as a sovereign nation. But the national celebration proved to be short-lived. As the Russian army's wave of violence receded, investigators soon discovered mounting evidence of the atrocities they left behind. At the same time, millions of uprooted Ukrainian women and children fled to neighboring countries, creating Europe's worst refugee crisis since World War II.

CHAPTER 10
THE HUMAN FRONT: ATROCITIES AND REFUGEES

CHAPTER 10
THE HUMAN FRONT: ATROCITIES AND REFUGEES

On Friday, April 8, 2022, several thousand Ukrainian women and children packed into the Kramatorsk railroad station. Hundreds waited anxiously for a train that would evacuate them from an imminent Russian offensive in eastern Ukraine. But war is always brutal. Suddenly, two deadly Russian missiles slammed into the station.

The Russians armed their 21-foot-long missiles with banned cluster bombs that ejected smaller bomblets designed to kill and maim. They did. Video shot seconds after the explosives revealed searing images of bodies, blood-soaked luggage, and children's toys scattered on the platform. "There were people everywhere," one terrified eyewitness reported, "Torn-off limbs, flesh, bone, pieces of people everywhere."

The unprovoked attack claimed the lives of 60 people while wounding more than 110. The brutal slaughter of civilians was not an accident. Instead, it implemented a Russian strategy of terror that blatantly ignored international agreements prohibiting the targeting of civilians. Although Russian officials shamelessly denied any responsibility, remnants of one of the missiles had "for the children" in Russian painted in bold white letters.

The deliberate Russian campaign of atrocities and war crimes is having important consequences. It has strengthened Ukrainian resolve to resist the Russians and solidified Western moral outrage against Putin's "special military operation." The Russian onslaught has also triggered a massive refugee crisis by forcing millions of Ukrainians to flee their homeland and seek refuge in nearby countries.

HORROR IN BUCHA

On February 23, 2022, Bucha was a peaceful residential suburb located about 20 miles northwest of Kyiv. But four days later, life in the town irrevocably changed when Russian tanks suddenly appeared. Bucha now became a strategic base in the Russian plan to seize Kyiv.

Russian soldiers remained in Bucha for 33 days. The Ukrainian forces that liberated the town discovered gruesome scenes that one soldier described as "hell on earth." Corpses lay scattered in the streets. Many of the bodies were found with hands tied behind their backs, close-range gunshot wounds, and horrifying evidence of torture. Callous Russian soldiers piled over a hundred bodies into a mass grave.

During the subsequent weeks, investigators painstakingly uncovered the full extent of the carnage in Bucha. Officials identified 458 bodies, 400 of which bore the markings of horrific abuse. Survivors described living in constant fear. Many reported terrifying encounters in which the difference between life and death depended upon the random whim of undisciplined Russian soldiers who often "acted like savages."

The scars of Bucha's nightmare remain deep and visible. Most of the homes that once bordered Bucha's picturesque tree-lined streets are destroyed. Family members are still trying to piece together what happened to their loved ones. For example, Vadim knows that his father Alexi hid with four others in a basement garage. But the garage soon became a place of death. Neighbors have told Vadim that they heard shots, screams, and then silence.

The 20-year-old son visited the site with David Muir, anchor of ABC World News Tonight. As they shifted through the ash and charred wood, Vadim suddenly uncovered human bones that might belong to his father. Like other survivors of Bucha, Vadim cannot rest until there is justice for his father and his neighbors.

URBICIDE IN MARIUPOL

Mariupol is a port city located on the Sea of Azov, just 35 miles from the Russian border. It had a pre-invasion population of 440,000. The city's strategic location made it an important Russian military objective. Controlling Mariupol would allow Russia to link its forces in the Crimean Peninsula with those in the separatist region of Donbas to the north.

Russia began bringing death and destruction to Mariupol in early March 2022. Moscow's relentless bombardment was not solely designed to capture Mariupol; instead, Putin also intended his war machine's campaign of sustained and indiscriminate destruction to leave the city in ruins. Military strategists use the term "urbicide" to describe violence specifically intended to destroy an urban area.

Putin achieved his ruthless objective. Russia's relentless shelling destroyed 90 percent of Mariupol's buildings and killed at least 20,000 of its residents. A lack of food, electricity, sanitation, and medical care traumatized countless others. A distraught survivor described Mariupol as "a freezing hellscape riddled with dead bodies and destroyed buildings."

ATROCITIES IN MARIUPOL

Although wars are deliberately destructive, there are accepted international rules of conduct. For example, it is a war crime to intentionally target civilian infrastructure such as maternity wards, hospitals, and shelters. But this restriction did not deter Russia's campaign of terror and death in Mariupol.

On March 9, Russian forces targeted a building housing a maternity ward and pediatric hospital. The blasts killed 3 people and wounded at least 17 others. Outraged by this atrocity, President Zelensky asked the world, "What kind of a country is Russia, that it is afraid of hospitals and maternity wards and destroys them?"

One week later, Russian forces provided Zelensky with an answer to his question. The people of Mariupol took great pride in their ornate drama theater. Located in a small park in the center of the city, the theater's size and thick walls made it an ideal bomb shelter. Within a short time, as many as 1,200 civilians found shelter in the building's basement, hallways, and offices.

The theater's set designer clearly marked the building as a civilian shelter. He used white paint to inscribe the word "CHILDREN" in giant Cyrillac letters on the pavement both in front and behind the building. The huge letters could even be photographed by orbiting satellites.

This plea for mercy did not affect Russian pilots. On March 16, a Russian warplane targeted the theater with laser-guided bombs. The sudden explosion turned the shelter into a place of death and terror. As many as 600 innocent civilians lost their lives in the deadliest single strike since the war began.

"I SAW ALL THIS WITH MY OWN EYES"

Trying to make sense of the death and destruction in Mariupol challenged even the most seasoned reporters. Their photographs and stories captured aspects of the endless terror unleashed during the Russian siege. But powerful insights can also come from an unexpected source:

an eight-year-old boy named Yehor Kravtsov kept a diary describing what he saw. His simple drawings and short but powerful sentences capture his family's desperate struggle for safety in a besieged city.

Yehor began his journal while huddled with his mother and teenage sister inside a freezing basement in his grandparent's home. Tragedy suddenly struck when a Russian missile slammed into the house. Yehor's grandfather suffered severe wounds as he courageously pressed his body against the door to shield his family from the blast. He died eight painful days later. Yehor's diary provides a poignant description of the carnage inside their subterranean room: "My grandfather died. I have a wound on my back. The skin is ripped off. My sister has a cut on her head. My mum has flesh torn out of her arm and a hole in her leg." Undaunted by their injuries, the stricken family sang together as they bandaged their wounds.

Yehor's diary includes drawings of the fierce fighting taking place outside his shelter. He filled the pages of his blue book with pictures of tanks, helicopters, and corpses. He captured the impact of Russian airstrikes by drawing smoke billowing from nearby homes. Yehor assures us that, "I saw all this with my own eyes."

Yehor's diary did more than record the chaos around him; it also saved his family. His uncle worked as a photographer who documented the battle for Mariupol. After seeing his nephew's diary, he posted several pages online. Inspired by Yehor's story, a group of determined activists helped the beleaguered family escape from Mariupol.

Yehor and his family successfully reached Kyiv. Although safe, they had no place to live. Unknown to them, Tina Karol, a popular Ukrainian singer and actress, read excerpts from Yehor's now-famous diary at her concerts. Karol's manager located Yehor's mother and offered to buy the family a finished apartment in a quiet residential neighborhood outside Kyiv. Although the Russians took away Yehor's beloved Mariupol, they could not take away his future.

WHY IS RUSSIA SO BRUTAL?

The train station in Kramatorsk, the bodies in Bucha, and the theater in Mariupol have become synonymous with Russian war crimes. Violence and death occur in all wars. But why have the Russian forces embraced deliberate acts of gratuitous brutality? Why launch missiles to attack women and children at a train station? Why allow soldiers to throw hand grenades into cellars where unarmed civilians are hiding? And why use jets to target a theater sheltering hundreds of women and children?

The answers to these questions begin with the twisted reality created by Russian propaganda. Kremlin state television repeatedly describes Ukrainian leaders as "Nazis" and its defenders as "fascists." Putin's forces expected Russian-speaking people in eastern and southern Ukraine to welcome them as liberators. When this didn't happen, frustrated Russian soldiers began to show no mercy to "traitors" who defied their expectations.

But can Russia's violence be fully explained as the fury of a frustrated army? Macha Gessen, an outspoken Russian-American journalist and author, argues that Russian brutality is not completely mindless. He reminds his readers, "This is how Russia fights wars…The regime is trying to win this war by causing intolerable suffering to civilians."

Russia's longstanding military tactics support Gessen's contention. The strategy of using overwhelming firepower to deliberately destroy civilian infrastructure has deep roots in Russian military history. For example, Russian forces killed over one million Afghan civilians during the Soviet occupation from 1979 to 1989. By weaponizing destruction and civilian deaths, Putin hopes to spread chaos and fear that will undermine Ukrainian morale.

THE REFUGEE CRISIS

The Russian onslaught violently disrupted daily life across Ukraine. In the first three months of the war, Russian fired more than 2,150 long-range, precision-guided missiles into Ukraine. Many targeted civilian apartments. Thunderous explosions in the middle of the night rocked once-peaceful neighborhoods. Desperate to escape, panic-stricken families packed a few belongings into their cars and fled into the darkness. Horrified children sometimes saw bombs strike cars in front of them.

Putin's brutal invasion prompted Europe's largest refugee crisis since World War II. In the war's first week, over 1 million people sought refuge in Poland and other nearby countries. By the late summer of 2022 as many as 6 million Ukrainians left their country while another 7 million people were displaced within their homeland.

Nearly half of all Ukrainian children have been forced to flee their homes. Heartbreaking pictures of terrified children forced the outside world to confront a growing humanitarian crisis. Images of desperate mothers and children sparked an outpouring of compassion and help. An army of volunteers greeted refugees and provided them with food, blankets, toothbrushes, stuffed animals, and even cell phone SIM cards.

Generous citizens in Poland and across Europe opened their homes to help refugees.

"HOW COULD PEOPLE ATTACK CHILDREN?"

The Ukrainian crisis has had unanticipated consequences. Putin anticipated that the challenge of helping millions of refugees would frustrate and divide the NATO allies. But that didn't happen. Instead, the war prompted an outpouring of kindness and generosity."

Russian atrocities have accomplished more than unifying Europe; they have also unified the Ukrainian public against Russia. Asked by a reporter how she felt about Russia, a Ukrainian mother spoke for many in her country when she answered: "They are killers. I hate them. How could people attack children?"

CHAPTER 11

THE ECONOMIC FRONT: SANCTIONS AND ENERGY

CHAPTER 11
THE ECONOMIC FRONT: SANCTIONS AND ENERGY

Pushkin Square is a large open space located in central Moscow. On a normal shopping day, it is one of the busiest public squares in the world. But January 31, 1990, was not a normal shopping day. On that date, McDonald's opened a much-anticipated restaurant in Pushkin Square.

Eager customers formed a long line for a chance to taste "Big Maks," french fries, and milkshakes. After waiting for up to three hours, diners entered the largest McDonald's restaurant in the world. The facility's 600 employees amazed Muscovites by providing them with efficient and friendly service.

The opening of McDonald's became a powerful symbol of Russia's entry into the global economy. But Putin's unprovoked invasion of Ukraine severed Russia's ties to the West. On March 8, 2022, McDonald's announced it would halt all business in its 847 Russian restaurants. Over 1,000 multinational companies soon joined the Golden Arches in an unprecedented exodus that included such iconic brands as Apple, Nike, Disney, Microsoft, Netflix, IBM, Starbucks, and Coca-Cola.

The exodus of multinational companies did not occur in a vacuum. Led by the United States, about 40 North American, European, and Asian governments unleashed a coordinated campaign of sanctions designed to punish Russia for its illegal invasion of Ukraine. Although the barrage of economic restrictions did not stop Putin from waging war, they did have a significant impact on the Russian economy.

The sanctions have done more than impact Russia; they have also set in motion shock waves that have reverberated across an increasingly-integrated global economy. The costs of the war quickly became apparent as motorists paid higher prices for gasoline and grocery shoppers watched helplessly as food prices steadily rose. The mixed impact of sanctions in Russia, Europe, and America raised questions about their effectiveness, costs, and unexpected consequences.

"AN ECONOMIC NUCLEAR BOMB"

Sanctions are prohibitions and restrictions imposed on governments, corporations, and individuals. Following Putin's invasion of Ukraine, the United States and its allies imposed thousands of sanctions on Russia, making it the most sanctioned country in the world. New York Times columnist Tom Friedman called these sanctions "the economic equivalent of an economic nuclear bomb on Russia."

Friedman has a point. The massive arsenal of Western sanctions is intended to isolate Moscow from the global economy. Punishing sanctions have targeted Russia's banks, companies dependent upon Western technology, and wealthy oligarchs with close ties to the Kremlin.

Each day a global financial messaging system called SWIFT facilitates the exchange of trillions of dollars among banks, companies, and governments. SWIFT stands for Society for Worldwide Interbank Financial Telecommunications. Created in 1973 and based in Belgium, SWIFT links 11,000 banks and institutions in more than 200 countries.

On March 7, 2022, Western nations removed Russian banks from SWIFT. Russian companies thus lost access to the instantaneous communication provided by the SWIFT system. This restriction disrupted payments for the nation's valuable energy and agricultural exports.

The barrage of sanctions also extended the economic battlefield by banning the sale of strategic technology to Russia. As a result, global semiconductor exports to Russia collapsed by 90 percent. The shortage of advanced technology crippled the Russian airline and automobile industries. For example, the lack of spare parts forced the Russian national airline Aeroflot to ground planes while at the same time production at automobile plants plummeted by almost 65 percent.

A series of especially punitive sanctions targeted wealthy executives known as oligarchs. The penalties enabled Western governments to seize luxury apartments, mansions, and superyachts owned by many of Putin's close allies. For example, French authorities seized the Amore Vero ("True Love"), a 289-foot superyacht owned by one of Putin's key supporters. Valued at $120 million, the superyacht's luxurious features included a swimming pool, beauty salon, gym, indoor elevator, and seven suites designed to comfortably accommodate 14 guests.

THE GREAT SANCTIONS DEBATE

In a speech delivered in Warsaw, Poland, on March 26, 2022, President Biden confidently declared that "These economic sanctions are a new kind of economic statecraft with the power to inflict damage that rivals military strength. These international sanctions are sapping Russian strength." Less than one month later Putin defiantly insisted that "The strategy of economic blitzkrieg has failed." These two dueling declarations frame a growing debate over the effectiveness of sanctions.

Supporters of sanctions argue that they are powerful tools. The International Monetary Fund predicts that the Russian economy will shrink by 6 points in 2022. Other signs of distress in Russia include an inflation rate soaring over 12 percent and unemployment at about 10 percent. Jeffrey Sonnenfeld, a professor at the Yale School of Management, contends that these economic indicators support his view that "The Russian economy is reeling."

Skeptics counter that while sanctions have wounded the Russian economy, they have not crippled it. They point out that although the Russian ruble initially crashed it quickly regained its value. Journalists in Moscow and St. Petersburg report seeing grocery shelves stacked with food, restaurants filled with diners, and highways congested with rush hour traffic. In an unexpected return to normalcy, McDonald's locations across Russia have been replaced by a Russian-owned chain called "Tasty and That's It." One shopper in Moscow summarized a widely held belief when she told a New York Times reporter, "Nothing has really changed. Sure, the prices have gone up, but we can endure that."

FACTORS LIMITING THE SUCCESS OF SANCTIONS

Barring banks from SWIFT, banning the sale of high-tech semiconductors and seizing superyachts all battered the Russian economy. However, these measures failed to deliver the economic knockout blow predicted by Western governments. Patient Russian consumers tolerated rising prices and the shortage of cars and luxury goods. At the same time, Putin's grip on power remained firm as he continued to wage war against Ukraine.

What factors are limiting the success of sanctions? Analysts point out that crippling the world's 11th largest economy will require time. Furthermore, the refusal of China, India, Brazil, and many African countries to enforce restrictive embargoes has cushioned the blow to the Russian economy.

The size and complexity of the Russian economy and the lack of full international support has placed limitations on the effectiveness of Western sanctions. While important, they are not the most important factors preventing sanctions from working. The Putin regime's political and economic stability rests on the crucial energy sector.

Russia contains vast and valuable reserves of both oil and natural gas. These natural resources have enabled Russia to become the world's leading exporter of fossil fuels. Revenue from the sale of energy funds 40 to 50 percent of the national budget. The invasion of Ukraine caused a sharp spike in oil and gas prices. Windfall profits from soaring energy prices have buoyed the nation's economy and insulated it from the full impact of Western sanctions. As a result, Putin has been able to simultaneously fund his war machine and counter inflation with a generous 20 percent increase in government pensions.

GERMANY AND RUSSIAN ENERGY

For decades, Europe and especially Germany relied upon Russian energy to heat homes, power factories, and fuel vehicles. Germany is Europe's most industrialized and populous country. Although it is the continent's economic powerhouse, Germany is heavily dependent upon imported Russian oil and gas. At the beginning of 2020, Russia supplied 50 percent of Germany's natural gas and 35 percent its oil.

A combination of practical and idealistic factors contributed to Germany's dependence on Russian energy. Germany turned to Russian gas because it was easy to transport and readily available. At the same time, idealistic German leaders believed that a "trade bridge" with Russia would promote peaceful relations by building trust, cooperation, and beneficial mutual growth. German Chancellor Helmut Schmidt expressed this optimistic assumption when he confidently asserted that, "Those engaged in trade with each other do not shoot at one another."

The German conviction that peaceful trade made war unprofitable and irrational contributed to their decision to support construction of the Nord Stream 1 pipeline. Opened on November 8, 2011, the 10 billion dollar pipeline stretches 759 miles from the Russian coast near St. Petersburg to a terminal in northeast Germany. When functioning at full capacity, Nord Stream 1's 48-inch wide twin pipes can supply Germany with a daily equivalent of about 45 million gallons of natural gas.

"A SAFE AND RESILIENT PARTNERSHIP"

Led by Germany, the European Union became more and more reliant upon imported Russian energy. By 2021 Europe depended upon Russia for 25 percent of its oil and 60 percent of its gas. German leaders ignored American warnings about the risks of dealing with a single energy provider; instead, they discounted American concerns and agreed to partner with Russia on a second Nord Stream pipeline. German Chancellor Angela Merkel stressed her belief in the project by reaffirming her conviction that Europe and Russia would "remain linked in a safe and resilient partnership."

Putin's decision to invade Ukraine shattered the "safe and resilient partnership" between Europe and Russia. Germany promptly refused to certify the Nord Stream 2 pipeline thus killing the project. Putin responded to this and other Western sanctions by stopping the delivery of natural gas from the Nord Stream 1 pipeline. He hoped this embargo would weaken European solidarity and erode Western support for Ukraine.

EUROPE ON EDGE

Putin's strategy of weaponizing energy sales failed to pressure the European Union into abandoning Ukraine. However, it did plunge Europe into a precarious new era of economic uncertainty. Wary Europeans braced for a winter of soaring inflation, rising unemployment, and looming shortages of gas to heat their homes.

The unfolding energy crisis forced European governments to take emergency measures to prepare for the uncertain winter months. In an attempt to mitigate their reliance on Russian energy, EU members successfully filled their gas storage facilities to a level approaching 90 percent. They also turned to Norway to increase its gas exports. Consequently, this Scandinavian country has now replaced Russia as the EU's leading supplier of natural gas.

SHORTAGES AND ANXIETIES

President Biden warned Putin that the United States and its allies would unleash an unprecedented barrage of sanctions directed at the Russian economy. The sanctions failed to deter Putin from invading Ukraine. However, they did create shortages and anxieties among both Russians and Europeans.

Western sanctions changed but did not seriously disrupt daily life in Russia. Affluent Russians could no longer book flights to Europe while shoppers in upscale malls discovered that Guicci, Chanel, and Luis Vuitton had closed their stores. Meanwhile, working class Russians became increasingly anxious as inflation eroded their purchasing power and reductions in automobile manufacturing threatened their jobs.

The economic battlefield also extended to Europe. The sharp reduction in Russian energy imports caused a growing anxiety as the continent braced for winter shortages and possible blackouts. Concerned about the lack of gas to heat their homes, many Europeans began to purchase wood burning stoves. As a result, pallets of wood became prized commodities as Europeans prepared to return to the "old days" when families gathered around their fireplaces.

# CHAPTER 12

THE INFORMATION FRONT: PROPAGANDA AND MISINFORMATION

CHAPTER 12
THE INFORMATION FRONT: PROPAGANDA AND MISINFORMATION

Russian President Vladimir Putin's sudden decision on February 24, 2022, to invade Ukraine left Oleksandra feeling shocked and terrified. Like other residents of Kharkiv, she knew her city would soon be under siege. Located in northeast Ukraine just 20 miles from the Russian border, Kharkiv quickly became a target for the invaders. During the last week of February, Russian missiles brought death and destruction to neighborhoods throughout the city. "People were panicking," the 25-year-old single woman told a BBC reporter. "I was so scared."

As the ominous sound of air-raid sirens reverberated across Kharkiv, Oleksandra called her mother in Moscow. She tried to convey a sense of the horror taking place around her. Although Oleksandra knew there was nothing her mother could do to stop the bombs, she did expect understanding and comfort. Despite repeated conversations and even short videos, Oleksandra could not persuade her mother to understand that her daughter faced real danger and that the next home to be hit could be hers.

Oleksandra's mother did understand that some military action was taking place in Kharkiv. However, she calmly reassured her terrified daughter by explaining, "Russians came to liberate you. They're only targeting military bases."

Her mother's disregard for the truth baffled Oleksandra. It shouldn't have. She didn't understand that Putin's war in Ukraine is also a war on the truth. Russia has a long tradition of using propaganda or misleading information to deliberately blur the distinction between facts and falsehoods. Like most Russians, Oleksandra's mother watches a continuous stream of propaganda on state-controlled television news programs. The Kremlin uses propaganda as an essential tool to win the information war by persuading its citizens that attacking Ukraine is both necessary and justified.

"UNCLE VOVA, WE ARE WITH YOU!"

Winston Smith is the chief protagonist in George Orwell's dystopian novel 1984. As a citizen of Oceania, Smith learns three fundamental truths: "War is Peace, Freedom is Slavery, Ignorance is Strength." Engraved on a white pyramid outside the Ministry of Truth, these slogans form Oceania's official motto.

The nightmarish world of relentless propaganda in the fictional Oceania has become a reality in Putin's Russia. The Kremlin's propaganda machine does not provide impartial live coverage of the war in Ukraine. Oleksandra's mother did not see news clips of bombed apartment buildings in Kharkiv or the civilians killed while they stood in line waiting for a drink of water. Neither she nor anyone else watching state TV news saw images of the heartbreaking exodus of millions of Ukrainian mothers and children.

The Kremlin's propaganda is effective because Russians are exposed to it from an early age. Continuous repetition creates and reinforces its own reality. Russian children are taught to fight for their country and obey their leader. A widely viewed YouTube video shows a choir of Russian children singing that "there should be peace on earth." However, the children then qualify their call for peace by forcefully declaring, "But if the commander-in-chief calls us to the last battle – Uncle Vova, we are with you!" The "last battle" is an allusion to nuclear war while Uncle Vova is a popular nickname for Vladimir Putin.

"2 + 2 = 5"

Russia's Orwellian propaganda is not limited to children's songs. The Kremlin understands the importance of controlling what is taught in their public schools. One week after Russian troops invaded Ukraine, schools across Russia received an official lesson on how to teach the conflict. The lesson plan included a question-and-answer format beginning with, "Are we at war with Ukraine? Could this have been averted?" The official answer is: "We are not at war. We are conducting a special military operation, the goal of which is to contain the nationalists who are oppressing the Russian-speaking population."

The official curriculum also includes a carefully prepared virtual lesson on "Why the liberation mission in Ukraine is a necessity." Teachers are instructed to emphasize "the damages" NATO has inflicted on Russia. Showing a complete disregard for historical accuracy, the propaganda video declares that their country must protect Russian-speaking children who have been persecuted by the Nazi-controlled regime in Kyiv. The irony of stating that Ukraine, a country devastated by the Nazis in World War II and now led by a Jewish president, is actually a Nazi controlled regime provides a perfect distortion of reality.

These lessons illustrate that reality is whatever the Kremlin wants it to be. War thus becomes peace. Similarly, in Orwell's 1984, the Party also distorts the truth by teaching that "2 + 2 = 5." Without any fixed facts, only the supreme leader can define what is "truth." As the leader of the Free World, America must continue to be a nation in which 2 plus 2 still equals 4.

"WE ARE RUSSIANS, AND GOD IS WITH US"

Russia's aggression against Ukraine is not limited to tanks and missiles. It is also delivered by television. Russian state news programs reach a large portion of the population. They play a particularly decisive role in shaping the opinions of elderly viewers who live in small towns and are less likely to access unfiltered information.

What are the television news programs teaching their audience about the war in Ukraine? First and foremost, viewers learn that there is no war at all. Putin's propaganda machine has banned the use of the words "war," "aggressor," and "invasion." Deputies in the State Duma enforced these rules by passing a bill making the discussion of "fake information" about the conflict in Ukraine punishable by up to 15 years in prison. At the same time, the Kremlin shut down all independent media outlets.

State news broadcasts repeatedly justify the "special military operation" as a necessary means to defend the Russian-speaking population living in the Donbas. According to the official narrative these people endure constant persecution by the Nazi-led government in Kyiv. Although the Ukrainian government is responsible for this discrimination, they are in fact "puppets" of the "real enemy" – the United States and its NATO allies. As the leader of the "evil West," the United States is a devious superpower determined to thwart Russia's legitimate security interests in Ukraine.

An endless succession of commentators remind their viewers that Russians are a brave people resisting the threat posed by Nazis in Kyiv and sinister Americans in Washington. According to this widely accepted "us versus them" view of the world, today's Russians can be heroes much like the generation that defeated Nazi Germany. The host of a widely viewed news program regularly voices this conviction when he closes his broadcast by exhorting his audience, "We are Russians, God is with us. Victory will be ours!"

RUSSIAN TECHNIQUES OF MASS DECEPTION

The Kremlin propaganda machine shifts into high gear to explain wartime atrocities. On March 9, 2022, Russian jets bombed a hospital maternity ward in Mariupol. Devastating explosions left 3 dead and 17 badly wounded. One injured mother suffered a crushed pelvis and a detached hip. Surgeons frantically tried but failed to save either the mother or her child.

Photographs of the injured mothers and shattered building outraged public opinion throughout the world. Headlines denounced the bombing as "barbaric" and a "heinous war crime." President Zelensky's press secretary Juliia Mendel bitterly wrote that the bombing "exposed the full criminal depravity of the Russian army to the world."

Russian authorities promptly responded by drawing upon their arsenal of mass deception techniques. The Kremlin initially claimed that the hospital was in fact a military facility occupied by Ukrainian armed forces. Putin's press secretary insisted that "Russians never attack anyone first" and always conduct missions with "surgical precision" to avoid injuring innocent civilians. He further claimed that the bombing of the "alleged maternity hospital" was in fact faked by the Ukrainians in order to denigrate Russia. State television announcers repeatedly told their viewers that the dying mother was actually a paid actress.

The Russian response to the bombing of the maternity ward in Mariupol illustrates the Kremlin's key propaganda techniques of deception, deflection, and delay. First and foremost, Moscow unleashed what the Rand Corporation calls "a firehose of falsehood." Putin's spin masters use multiple explanations to deceive, create confusion, and sow public doubt. Second, their shameless willingness to disseminate lies deflects independent truth by fabricating an alternate reality in which there are no established facts. And finally, Russia never accepts immediate responsibility for its actions. Instead, Moscow poses as an innocent victim surrounded by malevolent adversaries, thus delaying any timely reckoning with the truth.

The Kremlin uses these techniques of mass deception, deflection, and delay to distract the Russian public and create a new reality where it is accepted that 2 + 2 = 5. As a result, lies become truth and are official policy. When this happens, war crimes like the bombing of the maternity hospital in Mariupol become inevitable.

RUSSIAN PUBLIC OPINION

Televised scenes of the war in Ukraine are often difficult for Western audiences to watch. Americans assume that carefully documented reports of atrocities would spark widespread public outrage inside Russia. But that assumption is wrong. The Kremlin's propaganda machine has successfully labeled negative stories as "fake news" and then mobilized public support for President Putin and his invasion of Ukraine.

The Levada Center is a respected and independent research organization located in Moscow. Levada's research specialists regularly conduct carefully constructed surveys designed to measure Russian public opinion. They also supplement these surveys by conducting focus group interviews with representative Russian citizens.

Levada polls have consistently found that 80 percent of the Russian public approves of Putin's job performance. This overwhelming support is not difficult to explain. Many Russians have known no other leader. In addition, Putin faces no challenges from political opponents or critical questions from a free press. As a student of history, Putin undoubtedly knows that these same techniques worked during Joseph Stalin's 30-year rule.

Survey reports identify three distinct attitudes towards the Russian military activities in Ukraine. Just under half of all respondents "definitely support" Russian military activities. This group of "true believers" is convinced their country has a responsibility to liberate Russian-speaking Ukrainians and "stand up" to hostile Western powers.

A second group comprising about 30 percent of the public "mostly supports" Russian military activities. This group believes that their government leaders know what is best. They dismiss atrocities as either "fake news" or "exaggerated reports." Lavada researchers believe that members of this group prefer to remain in a "psychological comfort zone" where their passive support for the war is "less a matter of conviction than conformism."

And finally, Levada surveys reveal that about 20 percent of their respondents do not agree with Russian activities in Ukraine. Young professionals who live in Moscow and St. Petersburg and have traveled to Europe dominate this group. Although they oppose the war, most believe that protests are pointless and ultimately futile. One discouraged critic of the war confided to members of his focus group, "I went to a rally, and what happened? Did it change anything? Yes it did – I was fired!"

"THEY'RE LYING TO YOU"

Marina Ovsyannikova privately wrestled with the moral questions that anguished other opponents of the war. As an editor at Channel One, a Russian state-run television station, she knew the truth about the conflict in Ukraine. But she also knew that defending the truth in Putin's Russia would require great courage and sacrifice. Outraged by the scale of death and destruction in Ukraine, Ovsyannikova chose to stage a bold protest.

As millions of viewers watched the evening news on March 14, 2022, Ovsyannikova suddenly appeared behind the female anchor and shouted: "Stop the war. No to war!" She also held a handwritten sign which when translated into English read: "Don't believe the propaganda. They're lying to you."

Prior to her dramatic public protest, Ovsyannikova recorded a video message explaining the reasons for her protest: "What is happening in Ukraine is a crime. Russia is an aggressor country and the responsibility for this aggression rests on the conscience of only one person. That person is Vladimir Putin…I've spent the last few years working on Channel One, doing Kremlin propaganda, and I'm very ashamed of this."

Ovsyannikova's bold protest marked the first-time viewers of Russia's tightly controlled news broadcast had been exposed to a dissenting view. Dissidents inside Russia praised her courage and conviction and hoped it would ignite a wave of protests.

Russian officials did not praise Ovsyannikova. A Kremlin spokesman dismissed her protest as "an act of hooliganism." Denied legal assistance, Ovsyannikova disappeared from public view while authorities interrogated her for 14 hours. Faced with the possibility of a long prison sentence, Ovsyannikova escaped from her pre-trial house and fled to Europe.

"LIVING THE TRUTH"

Kremlin propagandists are waging an information war to prevent the truth from reaching the Russian public. Given the very real threat of harsh punishments, speaking the truth requires great courage and a willingness to suffer severe personal and family consequences. It is often far easier to remain silent and accept that 2 plus 2 can equal 5.

Vaclev Havel provides an inspiring example of a leader who refused to passively accept the lies perpetrated by the Soviet puppet regime in Czechoslovakia. In a political essay written in 1978, Havel wrote: "If the main pillar of the system is living a lie, then it is not surprising that the fundamental threat to it is living the truth. That is why it must be suppressed more severely than anything else." Although he was imprisoned several times, Havel witnessed the fall of the Soviet Union and became his country's first democratically elected leader.

"Living the truth" in Russia is not easy. A peaceful, democratic, Putin-free Russia will require courageous dissidents who, like Vaclev Havel and Ovsyannikova, refuse to remain silent in the face of lies. People of courage and conviction must continue to believe that 2 plus 2 does equal 4, ignorance is not strength, war is not peace, and freedom is not slavery but instead is an inalienable right of all humans.

CHAPTER 13

MR. PUTIN'S WAR: APRIL – SEPTEMBER 2022

CHAPTER 13
MR. PUTIN'S WAR: APRIL – SEPTEMBER 2022

On September 10, 2022, enthusiastic throngs of Muscovites gathered across their city to celebrate the 875th anniversary of its founding in 1147. Russian President Vladimir Putin participated in the festivities by officially opening a 460-foot-high Ferris wheel. That night a spectacular fireworks display lit up the skies over Moscow's famed Red Square. Putin proudly declared that "Moscow is rightfully considered one of the most beautiful and comfortable megacities in the world."

Putin's speech conveniently ignored dramatic developments taking place on the battlefield in eastern Ukraine. While Putin opened Europe's largest Ferris wheel, Ukrainian special forces sliced through Russian lines in what only a few days before had been occupied territory south of Kharkiv. Caught by surprise, panicked Russian soldiers abandoned their weapons as they fled before the Ukrainian onslaught.

Russia's humiliating retreat created a new and unforeseen reality. Russian officials and many Western commentators assumed that Moscow's larger and better equipped forces would inevitably triumph. But Ukraine's lightning counteroffensive in early September cast doubt on this assumption.

Ukraine's stunning victories did more than shatter conventional assumptions; they also placed Putin in a strategic bind. He launched an unprovoked invasion to return Ukraine to Russia's sphere of influence and reestablish Moscow as a feared and respected great power. The embarrassing military setbacks threatened to undermine both objectives. Trapped on an unpredictable and unforgiving wheel of historic change, Putin now faced new and unforeseen challenges.

A GRINDING WAR OF ATTRITION

The first phase of the Russian invasion didn't go the way Putin predicted. The Kremlin expected to quickly topple the Zelensky government. As described in Chapter 9, Ukraine mounted a fierce resistance that foiled Putin's plan. In early April 2022, Russian commanders withdrew their forces from the towns surrounding Kyiv. After failing to capture the Ukrainian capital, Putin ordered Russian troops to regroup and use their firepower to gain full control over the Donbas.

Despite their setback in the battle for Kyiv, Russian forces continued to retain overwhelming advantages in armor, artillery, and missiles. For example, the Russian war machine enjoyed at least a 10-to-1 advantage in artillery and ammunition. The open fields and compact industrial cities in the Donbas favored these advantages.

As the war shifted to the Donbas, the odds seemed heavily stacked against Ukraine. During the long summer months, Russian artillery guns fired as many as 50,000 shells per day as the Kremlin's war machine slowly blasted its way from one town to another. The Russian high command's indiscriminate shelling demonstrated a callous lack of concern for collateral damage to Ukraine's civilian population. For example, intensive artillery bombardments completely destroyed Mariupol and killed thousands of civilians.

Ukraine's outgunned but tenacious army could not win a protracted and grinding war of attrition. President Zelensky grimly reported that his forces were losing 100 to 200 soldiers a day while also suffering injuries to another 500 troops. He warned that Ukraine could not indefinitely endure these losses. As the Russian artillery relentlessly pounded Ukrainian military and civilian targets, the optimism sparked by the victorious battle of Kyiv began to fade.

HIMARS AND THE PRECISION REVOLUTION

Ukraine's brave defenders needed more sophisticated weapons. Help began to arrive in early July when the United States shipped the first HIMARs to Ukraine. HIMAR is an acronym for High Mobility Rocket System.

The HIMAR is a potent weapon that combines deadly accuracy, impressive range, and rapid escape mobility. Each launcher holds six rockets that are loaded onto a pod attached to a dark green truck weighing 10,000 pounds. The GPS guided rockets carry a 200-pound warhead capable of traveling up to 50 miles and striking within 10 feet of an intended target. Although there are HIMAR rockets that have ranges up to 200 miles, the Biden administration drew a line by refusing to supply these longer-range missiles, fearing the Ukrainians would launch attacks at targets within Russian territory.

The HIMAR is not a "fire and forget" weapon but rather a fire and move system. When the HIMAR fires, its rockets leave a trail of exhaust that can give away the unit's position to enemy counterfire. Most artillery pieces are vulnerable because they must be towed by slow moving tracked vehicles. In contrast, the wheeled HIMAR truck can quickly move to another location at speeds up to 55 mph. This ability to "shoot and scoot" has made it almost impossible for the Russians to successfully target any of the HIMAR units.

The Ukrainian high command quickly put its new weapon to use. The HIMAR's lethal versatility caught the Russians by surprise. During the late summer, American intelligence satellites and Ukrainian reconnaissance drones provided HIMAR teams with a continuous stream of precise coordinates for high-value Russian targets. This enabled three-man HIMAR teams to target and destroy hundreds of Russian command posts, artillery batteries, electronic warfare systems, and ammunition depots.

The HIMAR's pinpoint strikes represent what military analysts call a "precision revolution." During the late summer of 2022, HIMAR rockets began to severely degrade the Russian forces. Putin would feel the full impact of these losses in early September.

A STUNNING UKRAINIAN COUNTEROFFENSIVE

The first days of September seemed uneventful, but appearances along the front lines south of Kharkiv were deceptive. "The Russians were acting as if this was their house," reported one Ukrainian commander. "They were way too comfortable. And they had no idea what was coming."

The Ukrainian officer was right. During August, Ukrainian officials and media broadcasters publicly touted the army's preparation for a large-scale operation to retake territory near Kherson, a strategic port city located hundreds of miles south of Kharkiv. The ruse worked. Worried Russian commanders repositioned troops to reinforce the defense of Kherson thus weakening their positions south of Kharkiv.

On September 6, 2022, Ukrainian forces shocked Russia and the world by launching a stunning counteroffensive in the region south of Kharkiv. Caught by surprise and lacking the will to fight, panicked Russian forces fled for their lives. They abandoned tanks, artillery pieces, and tankers filled with fuel. Within a week, Ukraine recaptured a vast swatch of Russian-occupied territory.

"OF COURSE, I'M HERE"

The sudden Ukrainian counteroffensive dealt the most devastating blow to Russian forces since their humiliating retreat from Kyiv. On September 14, President Zelensky underscored Ukraine's gains by making a surprise visit to Izyum, a strategic railroad hub that had served as an important Russian logistical base. Zelensky proudly watched as his soldiers raised Ukraine's blue and yellow flag over the ruins of buildings ringing the city's central plaza. "The heroes are here," he proclaimed. "We are moving in only one direction: forward toward victory."

Tragically, widespread death and destruction tempered the Ukrainian victory. Distraught survivors often stood in front of ruined apartment buildings that entombed the remains of their family and friends. The shattered limbs of wounded children testified to the brutal consequences of Russian land mines.

Although they suffered enormous hardships, Ukraine's people remained resolved to fight back. "They killed the man I love," a visibly shaken former television journalist told a New York Times reporter. Determined to avenge his death, she joined the Ukrainian military. "Of course, I'm here," she said simply.

PARTIAL MOBILIZATION

President Putin continued to promote Russia's armed forces as a symbol of national pride and power. But Ukraine's dramatic counteroffensive undermined his attempt to maintain an appearance of normalcy. The military's embarrassing retreat sparked rare criticisms of the Kremlin's official narrative lauding the "special military operation" as an unqualified success.

Influential criticism of the war did not come from the relatively small group of anti-war protesters outraged by Russian atrocities. Instead, opposition came from ultra-nationalists and fervent pro-war commentators incensed by Russia's battlefield failures. Although these groups did not directly criticize Putin, they did clamor for an escalation of the war against Ukraine.

Putin recognized the importance of silencing the war's critics and stabilizing the military situation. On September 21, 2022, he delivered a 14-minute address to the Russian people. Putin began by portraying Russia as a victim rather than an aggressor. He angrily warned that the

Western powers were using the "neo-Nazi" regime in Kyiv "to weaken, divide, and ultimately destroy our country."

Putin blamed Ukraine for "firing at hospitals and schools and staging terrorist attacks against peaceful civilians." He insisted that the "special military operation" remained committed to its primary objective of "liberating the whole of Dorbas." Putin then surprised his listeners by declaring a partial mobilization to call up as many as 300,000 reservists.

REACTIONS

The unexpected partial mobilization sent shock waves across Russia. Abrupt notifications gave eligible men an hour to pack their belongings and appear at draft centers. Shocked university students received draft notices while attending classes.

Confronted with the choice of fighting or fleeing, as many as 300,000 men of military age chose to leave Russia. Aerial photographs showed a 10-mile-long line of cars backed up at a border crossing with neighboring Georgia. Piles of abandoned bicycles served as stark evidence of panic among those determined to escape the draft. The exodus also spread to air travel. Soon after Putin's speech, tickets sold out to the few cities that continued to maintain direct flights from Russia. One-way tickets from Moscow to Istanbul remained scarce despite prices that skyrocketed to over $9,000.

The sudden departure of sons and husbands had a particularly devastating impact upon Russian women. Distraught mothers and wives complained that underequipped and undertrained soldiers were forced to eat moldy rations and dig trenches with their bare hands. They tried to help their loved ones by raising money to buy them boots, winter clothing, and night goggles.

"THIS IS NOT A BLUFF"

The conflict with Ukraine raged much longer than Putin anticipated. Confronted with humiliating setbacks, he chose to escalate the war by mobilizing 300,000 reservists. Instead of seeking an off-ramp to end the conflict, Putin concluded his address by warning, "In the event of a threat to the territorial integrity of our country and to defend Russia and our people, we will certainly make use of all weapon systems available to us." He underscored this ominous threat with the stark warning: "This is not a bluff."

Putin's veiled threat to use Russia's enormous arsenal of nuclear weapons had both strategic and psychological purposes. By stoking fear of a nuclear war, Putin hoped his tough rhetoric would deter America from sending Ukraine sophisticated tanks, advanced warplanes, and 200-mile long-range missiles. As a former KGB agent, Putin also understood the importance of using fear of a nuclear war to sow doubt and anxiety in the minds of the leaders and public in Western countries. He hoped that raising the specter of a nuclear war would force Ukraine and its partners into a premature peace agreement that would legitimize Russia's conquest of Ukrainian territory.

Putin's strategy of using nuclear blackmail did not intimidate President Zelensky or his military commanders. They understood that Putin's speech signaled that having chosen to start the war, he could not afford to lose it. Oleksiy Danilov, the head of Ukraine's National Security and Defense Council, emphasized that Putin remained a formidable adversary: "Russia has staked everything on this war. Putin cannot lose. The stakes are too high." Putin recognized that if his army returned to Russia in defeat, it would likely mean the end of his regime.

CHAPTER 14

FOREVER OR NEVER

CHAPTER 14
FOREVER OR NEVER

On September 30, 2022, hundreds of senior Russian lawmakers solemnly filed into St. George's Hall inside the Great Kremlin Palace. The hall's ornate marble columns, crystal chandeliers, and floor made from more than 20 types of rare wood all emphasized Russia's historic greatness and grandeur.

The audience did not have to wait long for what they knew would be a momentous ceremony to redraw the map of Eastern Europe. Russian President Vladimir Putin began by declaring that the week before millions of residents in four occupied Ukrainian territories had overwhelmingly voted to join Russia. Claiming the referendum represented the "will of millions of people," Putin bluntly warned "the Kyiv authorities and their real masters in the West to hear me, so that they remember this. People living in Luhansk and Donetsk, Kherson and Zaporizhia are becoming our citizens. Forever…Russia will not betray them." Putin and the four proxy leaders of these Ukrainian territories concluded the ceremony by holding hands and chanting "Russia! Russia! Russia!" to thunderous applause from the audience.

Western leaders promptly denounced the annexation as a brazen and illegal action. Ukrainian President Zelensky accused Russia of trying to "steal something that does not belong to it." President Biden condemned the referendum as an "absolute sham" in which many people reported being forced to vote at gunpoint. He vowed, "The United States will never, never, never recognize Putin's claim on Ukrainian sovereign territory."

The annexation ceremony marked a dangerous escalation in Moscow's war against Ukraine. It also represented a blatant attempt to use military force to change recognized international borders. The stark confrontation between Putin's pledge of "forever" and Biden's assertion of "never" appeared to close the door on diplomatic negotiations to end the war.

Within days a powerful Ukrainian counteroffensive in Kherson made the thunderous applause inside St. George's Hall seem a distant memory.

THE FALL OF KHERSON, MARCH 2022

Kherson is one of the four Ukrainian regions illegally annexed by Russia. Located in southern Ukraine, Kherson is roughly the size of Belgium. Rivers and irrigation canals crisscross the region's fertile farmland.

Kherson is more than a rich agricultural prize. The city of Kherson is a vital strategic location for both Russia and Ukraine. Located on the right or western bank of the Dnipro River, Kherson is an important Black Sea port and a gateway to the Russian occupied Crimean Peninsula.

The battle for Kherson began on February 24, 2022. Russian troops, tanks, and armored personnel carriers assaulted and captured the city in just six days. Kherson thus became the first and only Ukrainian regional capital seized by Moscow.

The Russian occupation quickly upended the lives of people living in Kherson. Life became grim as stores closed and food, medicine, and basic necessities disappeared from store shelves. Russian occupation officials pulled down Ukrainian flags and took over schools. At the same time, merciless Russian soldiers abducted and tortured hundreds of civilians in makeshift prisons euphemistically called "basements."

The harsh occupation did not deter Ukrainian opposition. One member of a resistance group vowed, "I wasn't going to work with them. Period!" He and his fellow insurgents ambushed Russian soldiers and transmitted the location of Russian military positions to Ukrainian artillery units stationed outside the city. Despite the threat of punitive reprisals, daring residents demonstrated their opposition by spray painting yellow ribbons on buildings and posts throughout the city.

THE LIBERATION OF KHERSON, NOVEMBER 11, 2022

The Ukrainian counteroffensive began on August 29, 2022. Armed with precision HIMAR long-range rockets, Ukrainian forces successfully targeted Russian command centers and ammunition depots. Ukrainian armored and infantry divisions simultaneously inflicted heavy casualties on Russian troops.

Facing a relentless Ukrainian advance, the Russian high command recognized that their forces inside Kherson faced an increasingly precarious situation. On November 9, 2022, Russia troops withdrew from the city and retreated to carefully fortified positions on the left or eastern bank of the Dnipro River. The river's wide waters now separated the two armies.

The first Ukrainian troops arrived in Kherson on November 11, 2022. Hundreds of jubilant residents raced to the city's central plaza to welcome their liberators. Freed from the brutal Russian occupation, they joyously waved their once-banned blue and yellow Ukrainian flags while shouting, "We waited for you! We love you!" The victorious soldiers autographed flags and tore down posters proclaiming the now defunct slogan, "Russia is here forever." One survivor spoke for many when he said, "We have no electricity, no water, no mobile connections, no internet connections, but we have no Russians and that's why we are so happy."

"IT IS IMPOSSIBLE TO KILL UKRAINE"

President Zelensky understood that the liberation of Kherson marked both an important strategic victory over Russia and a symbolic opportunity to rally Ukrainian morale. He ignored the objections of his security guards and in the early morning hours of November 14, 2022, embarked on a 9-hour train ride from Kyiv to Kherson.

Although they were still within range of Russian artillery, crowds gathered in Kherson's central square to welcome Zelensky. As usual, he refused to wear either a helmet or a bulletproof vest. His brief speech conveyed a deep conviction that Ukraine's enormous sacrifices would not be in vain. Zelensky admitted that the war was still far from over. However, he predicted that the recapture of Kherson marked "the beginning of the end of the war." He then defiantly declared, "It is impossible to kill Ukraine."

THE WAR ON INFRASTRUCTURE

Putin confidently ordered his war machine to invade Ukraine to showcase how far Russia had come since the collapse of the Soviet Union in 1991. But his "special military operation" proved to be neither swift nor triumphant. Instead, Russia's humiliating retreat from Kherson marked yet another defeat in a parade of military blunders that began with the failed attempt to capture Kyiv. Putin nonetheless remained convinced that Russia would ultimately succeed. NATO Secretary General Jen Stoltenberg warned his colleagues, "We should not make the mistake of underestimating Russia."

Stoltenberg's warning proved to be accurate. Unable to achieve victories on the battlefield, Putin unleashed an aerial assault on Ukraine's civilian infrastructure. Beginning in October 2022, Russia launched waves of missiles and armed drones at targets across Ukraine. The relentless bombardment severely damaged Ukraine's electrical grid and left millions of people without heat or running water.

Putin's cruel but calculated war on Ukraine's vital civilian infrastructure had a number of objectives. He believed the loss of heat and power would weaken Ukrainian morale. At the same time, Putin hoped to trigger a humanitarian crisis that would prompt another wave of refugees to seek shelter in already overburdened neighboring countries. This would increase the cost of supporting Kyiv and compel NATO leaders to pressure the Zelensky government to begin negotiations to end the war on terms favorable to Moscow.

"WE ARE READY TO LIVE WITHOUT LIGHT"

Putin's decision to weaponize winter forced millions of Ukrainians to live and work in freezing temperatures with only intermittent power, heat, and running water. The Russian assault tested, but did not break, Ukrainian resolve. Lacking electricity, doctors used flashlights to illuminate operating tables. Residents of apartment buildings routinely placed boxes filled with food, water, and even diapers in elevators in case the power suddenly went out and left people stranded.

The scale of destruction made quick repairs impossible. Ukrainian officials addressed the problem by creating thousands of makeshift public shelters. Known as "points of light," each location provided distressed citizens a warm place where they could sip tea, recharge their phones, and find companionship.

Although faced with the worst winter of their lives, Ukrainians remained resolute. A 25-year-old resident of Kyiv summed up her nation's unwavering spirit when she told a reporter, "We are ready to live without light, but not with the Russians."

"WHY? WHY? WHY YOU?"

Russian missiles and drones did not always strike infrastructure targets. In early December 2022, a barrage of rockets suddenly struck a small settlement along the banks of the Dnipro River on the outskirts of Kherson City. The village had no strategic value.

One of the rockets exploded in the yard outside Svitlana Zubova's small home. In a flash, the rocket exploded and killed her son-in-law Dmytro Dudnyk. The 38-year-old father of 8- and 13-year-old daughters had just brought his mother-in-law a chocolate bar to enjoy over tea. His last words were, "Mom, here's a chocolate bar for you."

Dmytro's sudden and senseless death provides a human face for the cruel impact of Russia's indiscriminate aerial assault on innocent civilians. In one terrible random moment, a family lost its father. Filled with unspeakable grief, Dmytro's wife wept at the side of his lifeless body as his distraught mother-in-law screamed at the sky, "Why? Why? Why you?"

"UKRAINE IS ALIVE AND KICKING!"

Ukraine's survival is not inevitable. Its resilient people are enduring bitter cold, dark nights without electricity, and random missile attacks on innocent civilians. Its courageous army is skillfully using advanced American weapons to shatter the myth of Russian military invincibility.

President Zelensky is successfully convincing his people and the Free World that Ukraine will prevail. On December 21, 2022, he stood before a special joint session of the U.S. Congress. Wearing his signature green battle fatigues, Zelensky thanked the United States for its military, financial, and humanitarian support. He presented House Speaker Nancy Pelosi and Vice President Kamala Harris with a battle flag signed by soldiers defending the besieged Ukrainian city of Bakhmut where he had just been the day before.

Zelensky proudly and defiantly proclaimed, "Ukraine is alive and kicking!" He further declared, "Ukraine holds its line and will never surrender." Zelensky's assertions were not based upon optimistic fantasies. Ukraine's opposition to Russia and to Putin is forming a strong national identity.

Zelensky concluded his address by characterizing Ukraine's struggle as the front line in a global battle for freedom and democracy against tyrants like Putin who are seeking to use violence to rewrite the international order. Zelensky is right. The ongoing war between Ukraine and Russia is part of a global struggle between the forces of democracy and autocracy. Although a long, grueling, and costly conflict remains, Ukraine is still standing.

CHAPTER 15
SIX LESSONS FROM THE UKRAINE WAR

CHAPTER 15
SIX LESSONS FROM THE UKRAINE WAR

Lincoln presented his Second Annual Message to Congress on December 1, 1862. Delivered less than three months after the fateful Union victory at Antietam and just one month before the announcement of the Emancipation Proclamation, Lincoln solemnly reminded the members of Congress, "We cannot escape history." Lincoln was right. Although we all live in the present moment, history is a living reality with enduring consequences.

The study of history does not provide us with an easily followed road map. Although aware of this limitation, this book attempts to provide readers with a framework for understanding the compelling leaders and dramatic events that have played key roles in the Ukraine War.

The war is still an ongoing story. It is possible nonetheless to discern six significant lessons beneath the breathless rush of headlines. It is important to emphasize that these "lessons" are not laws. However, they are linked to enduring characteristics of human nature and to repeating patterns found throughout history.

LESSON 1: LEADERSHIP MATTERS

History consists of stories, and stories must have villains and heroes. On February 24, 2022, Russian President Vladimir Putin gave the order for Russia's armed forces to invade Ukraine, thus plunging Europe into its largest land war since World War II. The invasion forced Ukrainian President Volodymyr Zelensky to make a fateful decision. He could accept an American offer to help him and his family escape to a safe location in Poland. Or he could remain in Kyiv. Zelensky chose to stay and lead his people.

Unforeseen events often change the course of history. Two days after Russian missiles began raining down on Kyiv, Zelensky boldly addressed the Ukrainian people. Standing in front of a well-known public building, he vowed to stay in Kyiv and fight on: "I am here. We will not lay down any weapons. We will defend our state, because our weapons are our truth." Zelensky's presence refuted the Russian disinformation that he had fled. He defiantly concluded by insisting, "It's our land, our country, our kids, and we will defend all of them. That's it. Glory to Ukraine!"

Zelensky's years as a popular television personality helped him understand the linkage between storytelling and political leadership. His short but forceful message offered his nation a compelling mission and purpose. Zelensky's courage and conviction lifted public morale and marked a key turning point in the war.

Zelensky did more than bolster Ukrainian morale; he also galvanized international support for his beleaguered country. During the spring of 2022 he spoke remotely to over 30 democratic parliaments and congresses throughout the world. Zelensky's message of freedom and democracy rallied political support and forged an emotional bond between Ukraine and the global community.

LESSON 2: APPEASEMENT DOESN'T WORK

Appeasement describes the policy of making concessions to a person or country in order to reduce tensions and avoid conflict. Appeasement seems like a rational and responsible way to use negotiations and compromise to resolve tensions and preserve the peace. But this is an illusion. In reality, appeasement doesn't work. Appeasement didn't stop Hitler from starting World War II and it didn't stop Vladimir Putin from launching an unprovoked and unjust war against Ukraine.

Like Hitler, Putin is a ruthless and immoral dictator. Undeterred by either the threat of sanctions or the promise of last-hour negotiations, Putin ordered the Russian war machine to invade Ukraine. Despite initial setbacks, Putin redoubled his campaign against Ukraine. In September 2022, he formally annexed four regions in eastern and southern Ukraine, ordered a mobilization of 300,000 additional soldiers, and threatened to use nuclear weapons. Alarmed by these actions, some Western leaders and political commentators advocated a policy of appeasement to avoid driving a dangerous Putin into a corner. Led by French President Emmanuel Macron, these self-proclaimed "realists" advised providing Putin with a "face-saving off-ramp."

The proposed off-ramp would trade Ukrainian land for peace. In this scenario, Russia would agree to a cease-fire in exchange for at least some of the territory it illegally annexed. The settlement would end a costly war and return peace and stability to Eastern Europe.

The off-ramp strategy is another name for appeasement. It overlooks Putin's horrific atrocities and rewards his aggression with territorial gains. It also ignores his core strategic outlook. Lenin advised Soviet leaders to "Probe with a bayonet: If you find mush, you push. If you find steel, you withdraw." Like Lenin, Putin only understands the language of power.

Putin has not asked for an off-ramp. He acts according to the logic of his historic mission. In Putin's mind, Russia cannot fulfill its destiny of becoming a strong, respected, and feared country without bringing all of Ukraine under its control. Historian and journalist Anne Applebaum rejects the notion that Putin needs an off-ramp. She forcefully argues, "He needs to lose. And only when he loses – only when he is humiliated – will Russia's wars of imperial conquest finally come to an end."

LESSON 3: HUBRIS LEADS TO NEMESIS

Hubris is a timeless and universal human trait. The ancient Greeks defined hubris as a false pride that leads to an attitude of supreme arrogance. Russian President Vladimir Putin's hubris began with his successful seizure of the Crimean Peninsula in 2014 (See Chapter 7). Undertaken over the objections of his closest advisors, this bloodless triumph confirmed Putin's confidence in his own infallible judgment. Intoxicated with success, Putin now believed that nothing was beyond his grasp.

Ambition is usually fueled by a desire for wealth and power. By 2022, Putin already ranked as one of the world's wealthiest men and Russia's undisputed ruler. Supremely self-confident, Putin began to focus more and more on his legacy as a historic Russian leader. In his mind, returning Ukraine to Russia's sphere of influence would elevate him into the company of Peter the Great, the 18th century czar who transformed Russia into a major European power.

Blinded by his ambition, Putin became a prisoner of his hubris. Now convinced of his own strategic brilliance, he confidently ordered the Russian army to invade Ukraine on February 24, 2022. But Putin overestimated the power of his forces and underestimated Ukraine's commitment to defend its independence.

Putin expected a "short victorious war." His false pride led him to ignore the inescapable price of hubris. In Greek mythology, hubris is inseparable from Nemesis, the goddess of vengeance charged with punishing a human filled with self-pride.

The Russian invasion quickly turned into a strategic quagmire. Although outgunned and outmanned, Ukraine's heroic defenders used advanced Western weapons to often defeat Putin's overconfident and unprepared army. Putin's hubristic dream of becoming a modern Peter the Great unraveled and quickly became a costly nightmare.

LESSON 4: PUTIN IS BLUFFING

Russian President Vladimir Putin is a former KGB agent who understands how to use fear to manipulate his opponents. He has been deliberately rattling Russia's nuclear sabers throughout the conflict with Ukraine. When the invasion began, Putin warned that any outside interference would lead to consequences "never seen in history." After a series of humiliating battlefield losses, Putin once again resorted to threatening nuclear rhetoric by declaring that "Russia will use all the instruments at its disposal to counter a threat against its territorial integrity. This is not a bluff."

As Russia's commander-in-chief, Putin has control over a formidable nuclear arsenal. The Russian nuclear stockpile contains at least 1,500 strategic missiles capable of reaching and destroying cities in America. The Kremlin's arsenal also includes just under 2,000 smaller but still destructive tactical nuclear warheads. Much less powerful than intercontinental ballistic missiles, these tactical weapons have a range of just over 300 miles.

Putin's veiled nuclear threats have successfully unsettled the Biden administration and some of its NATO allies. President Biden has followed cautious policies designed to avoid needlessly provoking Putin. As a result of this restraint, the United States has thus far opposed sending Ukraine powerful offensive weapons such as jet fighters and long-range missiles.

The West's self-deterrence ignores three reasons why Putin's nuclear saber-rattling is a bluff. First and foremost, tactical nuclear warheads have only limited battlefield use. What target would Russia attack? Ukrainian troops are distributed along a line of defensive positions that stretch for over 600 miles. As a result, they are not concentrated in a few areas where a tactical nuclear strike would inflict significant war-changing casualties.

Second, breaking the nuclear taboo would unleash a tidal wave of global outrage. Key Russian allies such as India and China have expressed strong opposition to the use of nuclear weapons. An unprovoked nuclear attack would thus isolate Russia from the international community.

And finally, the United States has warned Putin that any use of nuclear weapons would "meet with catastrophic consequences." Although the United States and its allies have not publicly spelled out these consequences, many military strategists believe NATO could use its potent air force to sink the Russian Black Sea Fleet and overwhelm Moscow's already weakened ground forces.

Thus far these three obstacles have formed an effective barrier to deter Putin from a reckless roll of his nuclear dice. Instead, he will continue to use nuclear saber-rattling to sow fear. Although unnerving, these threats are a bluff and should not prevent the West from sending Ukraine the weapons its army needs to repel the Russian invaders.

LESSON 5: SANCTIONS HAVE LIMITATIONS

Reports from St. Petersburg, Russia, indicate that container ships filled with imported goods no longer steam into the city's now-empty docks. Supporters of sanctions point to this as evidence that Western sanctions are working. However, the impact of sanctions is being mitigated by a long line of trucks in Georgia, a country located thousands of miles south of St. Petersburg.

Georgia is a small, formerly Soviet republic that is home to 3.6 million people. Located along the eastern shore of the Black Sea, Georgia shares a mountainous border with Russia. During the first months of 2023, visitors and journalists reported seeing an enormous line of over 1,000 fully loaded trucks backed up behind a checkpoint at Georgia's border with Russia. The trucks are carrying a myriad of goods including car parts, industrial materials, and chemicals.

The empty docks in St. Petersburg and the long line of trucks in Georgia provide two contrasting images of how sanctions are and are not working. Proponents of sanctions argue that they are slowly but surely causing Russia to experience a prolonged and painful recession. But critics counter that the threat of sanctions failed to deter Putin from invading Ukraine. In addition, the West's unprecedented sanctions have thus far failed to cripple the Kremlin's ability to wage and finance its war against Ukraine.

The line of trucks waiting to enter Russia provides a vivid example of the Kremlin's ability to circumvent sanctions. But it is not the only loophole. As European demand for Russian oil has begun to shrink, Moscow lowered prices and pivoted to eager buyers in India and China. These two countries now purchase about 40 percent of Russian oil exports. As a result, Putin remains able to continue financing his war with Ukraine.

Sanctions are a signal of Western resolve to stand with Ukraine. However, they have not brought the Russian economy to its knees. The war thus continues to grind on with no end in sight.

LESSON 6: FLAWED ASSUMPTIONS LEAD TO FAULTY INTELLIGENCE

What do intelligence agencies in Russia and the United States have in common? Both countries invest vast sums of money to fund large and often secret organizations tasked with gathering information about their global adversaries. Despite their size and resources, both Russian and American intelligence operations have generated flawed but widely believed assumptions about Ukraine. Their faulty intelligence assessments have played a crucial role in miscalculations that have shaped the war in Ukraine.

Putin regards Ukraine as a vital item of "unfinished business." Convinced that Ukraine "has never had its own authentic statehood," Putin underestimated the country's growing spirit of nationalism. Given a false picture of Ukraine and propelled by his own unbridled hubris, Putin blindly ignored the risks of invading Ukraine.

Assessing Putin's actual intentions initially posed a challenge. French, German, and even Ukrainian intelligence agencies all misjudged Putin's objectives. They believed he was using a military buildup as a psychological ploy to intimidate Ukraine into making territorial concessions in the Donbas. In contrast, the United States drew upon its advanced signal intelligence and photo reconnaissance to privately and then publicly warn that a Russian invasion was imminent.

Although American officials correctly predicted the Russian invasion, the strength of Ukrainian resistance caught them by surprise. The collapse of the Afghanistan National Army, trained and equipped by Americans, deeply embarrassed the Pentagon. With the Afghanistan experience fresh in their minds, U.S. military commanders expected the supposedly powerful Russian war machine to overwhelm the Ukrainian defenders. As a result, the Biden administration hesitated to send Ukraine the heavy weapons its army desperately needed.

Russia and the United States possess the world's most elaborate intelligence agencies. Yet, Ukraine's fierce will to fight caught both by surprise. At first, American officials failed to grasp how poorly Russian troops would perform and how heroically Ukrainian troops would fight. They forgot that war is more than a contest between advanced weapon systems. In the end, the human will to fight for freedom can still be decisive. Thus, the lesson of Ukraine has become a story of a courageous fight for global democracy.

KEY PEOPLE, PLACES, AND TERMS

APPEASEMENT
The policy of making concessions to a person or country in order to reduce tensions and avoid a conflict.

ARTICLE 5
NATO's founding document states that any attack on an alliance member in Europe or North America "shall be considered an attack against them all."

BALTIC STATES
Geopolitical term used for Estonia, Latvia, and Lithuania. All three countries are members of NATO.

BUCHA
Suburb of Kyiv that has become a symbol of Russian atrocities.

CONTAINMENT
America's Cold War policy of blocking the expansion of Soviet influence.

CRIMEAN PENINSULA
A peninsula located along the northern shore of the Black Sea. Russia seized the region in 2014.

DONBAS
A heavily industrialized region in eastern Ukraine. It includes both the Luhansk and Donetsk provinces. Became the scene of heavy fighting in 2014.

MIKHAIL GORBACHEV
The eighth and final leader of the Soviet Union from 1985 to the country's final dissolution in 1991.

HIMAR
An acronym for High Mobility Rocket System. Each HIMAR launcher holds six rockets. It is a potent weapon system that combines deadly accuracy, range, and rapid escape mobility.

HUBRIS
A false pride that leads to an attitude of supreme arrogance.

JAVELIN
A portable anti-tank weapon that has played a significant role in destroying Russian tanks.

GEORGE KENNAN
Widely regarded as the creator and leading advocate of America's policy of containing Soviet expansion. Kennan later opposed the expansion of NATO.

LEONID KRAVCHUK
Served from 1991 – 1994 as Ukraine's first democratically elected president.

LEONID KUCHMA
Served from 1994 – 1999 as Ukraine's second president.

KYIV
Capital and most populous city in Ukraine.

LITTLE GREEN MEN
Masked Russian soldiers wearing unmarked green uniforms who led the takeover of the Crimean Peninsula.

MAIDAN
Central square in Kyiv. Site of major demonstrations during the Orange Revolution and the Revolution of Dignity.

MEZHYHIRYA
Lavish presidential residence built by Viktor Yanukovych.

NATO
An acronym for North Atlantic Treaty Organization. Founded in 1949, the alliance was founded to safeguard the freedom and security of its member nations.

NEMESIS
The Greek goddess of vengeance charged with punishing a human whose self-pride offends the gods.

OLIGARCH
Very wealthy business leaders who exercise significant political influence in Russia and Ukraine.

ORANGE REVOLUTION
A series of protests that took place in Ukraine from late November 2004 to January 2005. The demonstrators protested extensive corruption, voter intimidation, and electoral fraud in the 2004 presidential election. The Ukrainian Supreme Court ordered a revote that led to the election of Viktor Yushchenko.

PETRO POROSHENKO
Ukraine's fifth elected president. He served from June 2014 to May 2019 and presided over the initial stages of the Russo-Ukraine War.

PROPAGANDA
Misleading information designed to deliberately blur the distinction between facts and falsehoods.

VLADIMIR PUTIN
Russian politician and former intelligence officer who has served as the president or prime minister of the Russian Federation from 1999 to the present.

RED LINE
A defined limit to the actions that a nation is prepared to accept from another state.

REVOLUTION OF DIGNITY
Also known as the Maidan Revolution. The Revolution of Dignity took place in February 2014. Deadly clashes between protestors and government security forces culminated in the ousting of the pro-Russian president Viktor Yarukovych.

SANCTIONS
Economic prohibitions and restrictions imposed on governments, companies, and individuals.

SEVASTOPOL
Largest city in Crimea and the home port of the Russian Black Sea Fleet.

SPECIAL MILITARY OPERATION
Vladimir Putin's officially approved name for the Russian war in Ukraine.

SWIFT
An acronym for Society for Worldwide Interbank Financial Telecommunications. SWIFT is a global messaging system that facilitates the exchange of trillions of dollars among banks, corporations, and governments.

URBICIDE
Violence specifically intended to destroy an urban area.

VIKTOR YANUKOVYCH
Corrupt oligarch elected president of Ukraine in 2010. He fled to Russia in 2014 during the Revolution of Dignity.

BORIS YELTSIN
President of the Russian Federation from 1991 to 1999.

VIKTOR YUSHCHENKO
Third elected president of Ukraine. He took office following the Orange Revolution. However, political infighting and a sharp economic recession eroded his popularity.

VOLODYMYR ZELENSKY
A popular comedian and actor. Inaugurated as Ukraine's 6th president on May 20, 2019. Zelensky is now regarded as a global symbol of freedom and resistance to Russian aggression.

Made in United States
Orlando, FL
03 March 2023